W9-AWS-306

‹ CHILE ›

PLACES AND PEOPLES OF THE WORLD

CHILE

Christopher Dwyer

CHELSEA HOUSE PUBLISHERS
New York • Philadelphia

COVER: Chile's varied geography includes not only mountains and deserts but also this waterfall in Payne National Park.

Chelsea House Publishers
Editor-in-Chief: Nancy Toff
Executive Editor: Remmel T. Nunn
Managing Editor: Karyn Gullen Browne
Copy Chief: Juliann Barbato
Picture Editor: Adrian G. Allen
Art Director: Maria Epes
Manufacturing Manager: Gerald Levine

Places and Peoples of the World
Editorial Director: Rebecca Stefoff

Staff for CHILE
Associate Editor: Ellen Scordato
Copy Editor: Philip Koslow
Deputy Copy Chief: Nicole Bowen
Editorial Assistant: Marie Claire Cebrián
Picture Researcher: Joan Kathryn Beard
Assistant Art Director: Loraine Machlin
Designer: Debora Smith
Production Coordinator: Joseph Romano

5 7 9 8 6

Library of Congress Cataloging-in-Publication Data

Dwyer, Chris.
Chile / Chris Dwyer.
p. cm. — (Places and peoples of the world)
Includes index.
ISBN 0-7910-1102-X
1. Chile—Juvenile literature.   I. Title.   II. Series.
F3058.5.D88   1989
983—dc20   89-1028
CIP
AC

◄ C O N T E N T S ►

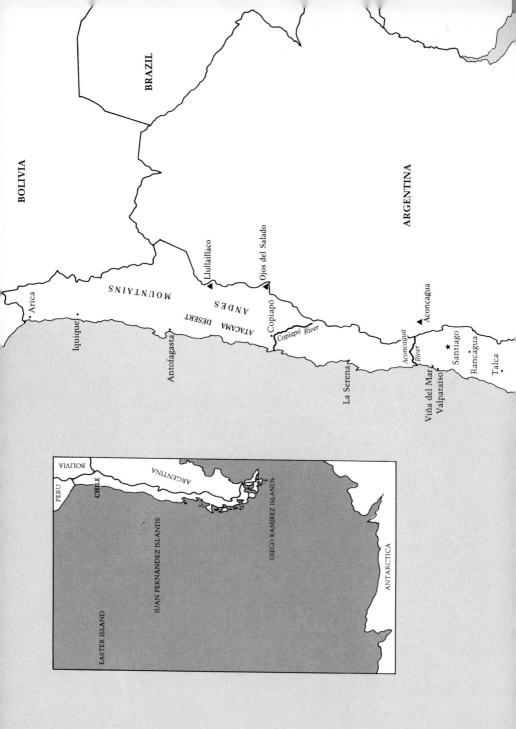

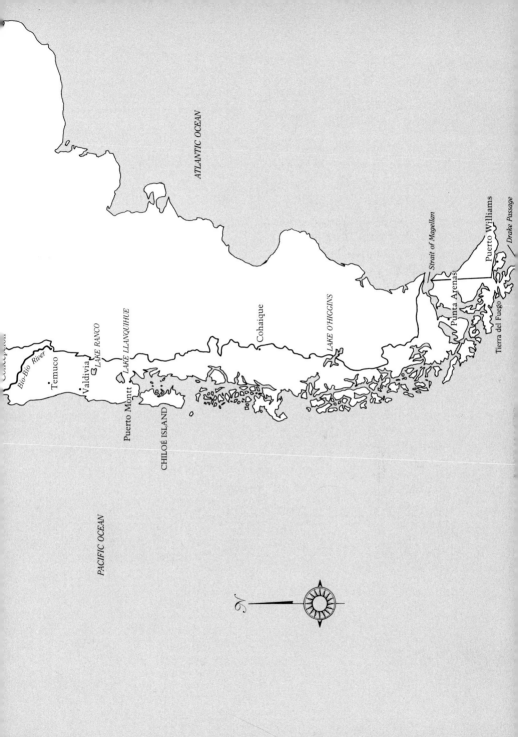

◄ FACTS AT A GLANCE ►

Land and People

Area 292,257 square miles (756,626 square kilometers); also claims 483,000-square-mile (1,250,000-square-kilometer) section of Antarctica, parts of which are also claimed by Argentina and Britain

Highest Point Ojos del Salado, 22,572 feet (6,772 meters)

Major Rivers Bío-Bío, Aconcagua, Copiapó

Major Lakes Ranco, Llanquihue, O'Higgins

Capital Santiago (population 4,804,200)

Other Major Cities Viña del Mar, Valparaíso (population 715,779), Concepción (population 714,521)

Population 12,866,000

Population Density 44 people per square mile (17 people per square kilometer)

Population Distribution Rural, 17 percent; urban, 83 percent

Official Language Spanish

Ethnic Groups Mestizo, 80 percent; European (mostly Spanish) and Middle Eastern, 18 percent; Indian (mostly Mapuche), 2 percent

Religions Roman Catholic, 82 percent; Protestant, other religions, and nonreligious, 18 percent

Average Life Expectancy 67.1 years

Economy

Chief Exports	Copper ores, unrefined and refined copper and other metals, fruits and vegetables, fish meal
Chief Imports	Machinery and transport equipment, fuels, food, chemicals and related products
Chief Agricultural Products	Sugar beets, wheat, grapes, potatoes, corn, apples, beans, rice, barley, oats, tomatoes
Land Use	Forested, 21 percent; meadows and pastures, 16 percent; agricultural and under permanent cultivation, 7 percent; other, 56 percent
Industries and Manufactured Goods	Mining, automobile assembly, fish and shellfish canning, cement, cellulose, sugar, newsprint, detergent, margarine, beverages, tires, plate glass, cigarettes, beer
Employment Statistics	Services, 35 percent; manufacturing and construction, 19 percent; trade, hotels and restaurants, 19 percent; agriculture, forestry, fishing, 18 percent; other, 9 percent
Currency	Peso, divided into 100 centavos
Average Annual Income	Equal to U.S. $1,465

Government

Form of Government	Military regime
Head of State and Head of Government	Major General Augusto Pinochet Ugarte, president, assisted by a four-member junta
Governmental Body	Ministers of state, appointed by president; 13-member Supreme Court, appointed by president
Local Government	Governors (appointed by president) control each of 12 regions; regions are subdivided into 42 provinces, controlled by *intendentes* (chief administrative officials) appointed by president; subdelegates oversee municipalities; mayors and city council members make up municipal government

◄HISTORY AT A GLANCE►

before 1500   Between 500,000 and 1,000,000 Indians live in the area that is now Chile. Although all are called Araucanians by later settlers, the primary groups are the Picunche in the central region, the Mapuche in the south-central region, and the Huilliche in the Far South.

1520   Portuguese navigator Ferdinand Magellan, sailing under the flag of Spain, sails from the Atlantic Ocean into the Pacific through a passage near the tip of South America. His men become the first Europeans to sight the coast of Chile.

1536   Diego de Almagro, Spanish conquistador and associate of Pizarro in the conquest of Peru, heads the first exploration of Chile by a European.

1541   Spanish adventurer Pedro de Valdivia claims Chile in the name of the Spanish king and gives his companions the right to demand tribute from the Indians.

1541–53   Valdivia pushes south into Chile's frontier. He sets up forts and settlements, including Santiago and Concepción. Valdivia is captured and executed by the Indians in 1553.

1600–1630s   Spanish settlers again try to penetrate Indian territory to the south, losing many battles to the fierce and clever Mapuche. The Spanish king begins payment of a *situado* (subsidy) to Chile to help maintain its government and army.

1646   The Pact of Quillon is signed between Spanish settlers and Chilean Indians—the only treaty in Spanish America that recognized Indian rights to control territory.

1655   After another attempt by Spanish colonists to settle in the region south of the Bío-Bío River, the Indians destroy all the Spanish settlements in the area.

1670s   The Jesuit order of the Catholic church wins the Spanish king's support for freeing Indian war prisoners and their children, but Indians who refuse to become Christians continue to be enslaved.

1700s   Changes in Spanish colonial policies include permission for free trade by Chilean merchants and the expulsion of the Jesuits from Spanish America in 1767.

1808–10   Napoleon's conquest of Spain encourages a number of Spanish colonies, including Chile, to declare independence from their parent country.

1814   Spanish troops defeat Chilean independence forces at the Battle of Rancagua to retake the country on behalf of the king.

1814–17   Chilean patriot Bernardo O'Higgins, in exile in Argentina, plots the recapture of Chile from the Spanish with Argentine liberator José de San Martín.

1817   After crossing the Andes, San Martín's forces defeat the Spanish outside Santiago. O'Higgins is named supreme dictator of Chile.

1818–30   A succession of governments in a variety of forms rules Chile. Liberals and Conservatives emerge as the main factions.

1830–37   After civil war leaves the Conservatives in power, Diego Portales, a government minister and private citizen, rules Chile in a virtual dictatorship.

1840–61   Chilean education improves with the founding of the University of Chile and the formation of a class of intellectuals and reformers who are influential in the new Liberal party, which comes to power in 1861.

1861–79   The introduction of railroads, the telegraph, and steamships encourages economic growth. Chilean workers travel north to work in nitrate fields and railroad projects in Bolivia and Peru, where Chilean companies have economic interests.

1879–83   Chile fights Peru and Bolivia in the War of the Pacific. Chilean forces occupy Lima, Peru's capital, obtain a surrender, and take over Peruvian and Bolivian provinces containing valuable nitrate fields.

1886–91   Following victory in the War of the Pacific, President José Manuel Balmaceda forces a constitutional crisis and brief civil war by refusing to cooperate with Congress.

1891–1920 Congress becomes much stronger after winning the civil war against Balmaceda. New political parties arise representing the middle and lower classes, workers stage strikes, and economic conditions deteriorate.

1920–31   Rising prices and the Great Depression cause misery and political turmoil as a succession of governments seize and then lose power.

1932–64   Legitimate, nonviolent changes of government take place. Education and culture develop. Three major political divisions form: the conservative right, the socialist left, and the moderate Christian Democrats.

1964 Christian Democrat Eduardo Frei, supported by the U.S. government, wins the presidential election over Socialist Salvador Allende.

1965–70 Frei implements the Revolution in Liberty, a program designed gradually to turn foreign-owned industry over to Chile and to redistribute land. Significant improvements occur in primary and secondary education.

1970–73 Allende wins the presidency by a narrow margin and embarks on the Chilean Road to Socialism, a program of government ownership of industry, land reform, and higher wages. Economic difficulties cause widespread dissatisfaction and strikes.

1973 The military seizes control of the government in a coup, after which a four-member junta headed by army chief of staff General Augusto Pinochet Ugarte takes power.

1973–78 Politicians, academics, and others who disagree with Pinochet's policies are brutally repressed. Thousands are tortured and killed in the Pinochet government's "holy war" on Marxism.

1980 A new constitution sets up formal military rule and extends Pinochet's term potentially through 1997.

1986 Guerrillas attempt to assassinate Pinochet. The government responds with further repression of antigovernment leaders, causing an international outcry.

Late 1980s Pinochet is voted out in October 1988 and must give up the presidency in March 1990.

‹CHILE›

A young boy gazes at the jumble of houses that climb the hills around Valparaíso. More than 700,000 Chileans live in the thriving city, which is the nation's principal port.

Chile and the World

The Republic of Chile is the long, narrow country that stretches along the southern Pacific coast of South America. Natural barriers define its borders. On the east, the majestic Andes Mountains separate Chile from Argentina and Bolivia; a smaller mountain range runs down the Pacific coast. The north, although rich in copper and other minerals, is mostly desert—many scientists consider it the driest place on earth. This bleak terrain extends into Peru, Chile's neighbor to the north. The southern part of the country, which contains valuable petroleum reserves and offers abundant fishing, splinters into a remote and isolated chain of storm-lashed islands.

Because of these geographic limits, the majority of Chile's 12,866,000 people live in the cities and farmlands of the central temperate region. This region begins at the Aconcagua River, just north of the capital city of Santiago, and continues southward between the Andes and the coastal mountains for 600 miles (965 kilometers) to the Bío-Bío River.

Chile appeared often in headlines and news broadcasts around the world during the 1980s. Controversy and conflict surrounded the strict rule of its president, Major General Augusto Pinochet Ugarte, who came to power in 1973 in a military takeover that was supported by the U.S. government. Pinochet and his followers seized power suddenly and violently in a *coup d'état*, or seizure of power, in which the elected president, Salvador Allende Gossens, was killed in an attack on the presidential palace. Pinochet's military supporters tortured and killed thousands of those who had supported Allende. Then, for 15 years, the Pinochet government used the same brutal tactics to fight Communism wherever it was known or even suspected to exist in Chile and also to quiet any disagreement with Pinochet or his policies. But in October 1988, Chile made news of another sort. The country held its first free election in 15 years. The election was a plebiscite, in which voters cast their ballots on a single issue: Should Pinochet be allowed to remain in office or not? Pinochet was voted out. He must allow free presidential elections and step down from office in early 1990. He has promised to do so, and many Chileans hope that his departure from the presidential palace will mean the end of military rule in Chile.

Unlike some other Latin American nations, Chile has seldom been under military rule since it achieved independence. Its recorded history begins in 1536–37, when the Spanish explorer Diego de Almagro became the first European to explore Chile. He withdrew after encountering fierce resistance from the native Indians. The next Spanish adventurer to try his fortune in Chile was Pedro de Valdivia. He arrived in the region in 1540 and later founded the cities of Santiago and Concepción. In 1551 he wrote that Chile "is rich in flocks as Peru, with wool that drags along the ground; abounds with all the foods that the Indians sow for their livelihood. . . . The land has a very fine climate and every kind of Spanish plant will grow in it better than over there." Two years after penning these optimistic words, Valdivia was killed by Indians.

His death, however, did not halt the Spanish expansion into Chile. Spain conquered the area, along with much of the rest of Central and South America, and ruled it as a colony for nearly three centuries. During this colonial period, Chile grew slowly; few Spanish people or other Europeans were eager to settle there. One reason for this reluctance was the formidable natural barriers that cut Chile off from the rest of the world, except for the Pacific Ocean. Another reason was that Chile lacked the immense wealth in gold and silver that the Spanish had plundered from Mexico and Peru. As a result, the Spanish kings and the powerful Roman Catholic church took little interest in this remote and unprofitable colony. They sent incompetent officials to govern it and required all of its trade to pass through the more important colony of Peru, where corrupt local officials seized large amounts of Chile's imports and exports in the form of bribes and other "taxes." This slowed Chile's development and made it an expensive place to live. Over the centuries, though, a profound disagreement gradually developed between the Spanish administrators of the colony and the Creoles, as those colonists who had been born and raised in Chile were called. Many of the Creoles began to feel that they should have more control over their own local government and less interference from far-off Spain.

The pace of events in Chile picked up in the early 1800s, when the French emperor Napoleon Bonaparte invaded Spain. Several of Spain's South American colonies took advantage of the confusion in their parent country to obtain their independence. Chile was one such colony. In 1817, the South American liberator José de San Martín, called the Knight of the Andes, gathered an army in Argentina, completed the difficult crossing of the Andes, and defeated Spanish forces outside Santiago. Chile was now an independent nation.

During the 1800s, the nation was governed under a constitution, with real power concentrated in the hands of the wealthy landowning class. European cultural influences became stronger; many Spanish, German, and French immigrants arrived to swell the population. Chile reached its present borders through military victories over Peru and Bolivia. The northern region that Chile won from these neighboring nations was a source of minerals, especially nitrates, which were used in making fertilizer and gunpowder. By the end of the century, Chile's economy depended upon the export of nitrates.

Despite General Augusto Pinochet's brutal repression of dissent during his 15 years in power, Chileans, who were accustomed to orderly transfers of power and a free press, repeatedly spoke out against his rule. These protesters attend the funeral of a 14-year-old boy killed in an earlier demonstration.

From 1920 to 1940, political disorder and economic upheaval gripped Chile. Governments changed quickly, sometimes under the threat of civil war or by means of violent takeovers, and some presidents were forced to resign. In addition, Chile's economy suffered when scientists around the world discovered how to manufacture an artificial substitute for nitrates. The worldwide Great Depression of the 1930s further ravaged the country, because other nations were unable to pay high prices for Chile's exports.

The 1940s brought more economic problems. The high cost of food and other goods led to riots and strikes by workers who demanded higher wages. At the same time, however, the government operated smoothly. Regular elections were held, and although power shifted frequently from one party to another, it did so without violence. By the early 1960s, many people considered Chile a model of civilized government—a place where the president could walk alone in safety from his house to La Moneda, the presidential palace.

Beginning in 1964, a change took place. Large numbers of voters turned to new political parties that sought to reform, or end, such features of Chilean life as the high cost of living, the foreign ownership of Chile's mines and industries, and the unequal distribution of land. Among these parties were several left-wing, or leftist, groups. (In political science, parties that favor conservative or moderate policies, with little government involvement in society and the economy, are often called rightist, or right-wing, parties; such parties may represent the interests of large businesses or of the upper classes. Parties of the left, on the other hand, traditionally favor government action to regulate social and economic programs, and they may be influenced by socialist, or, in some cases, communist theories of government and economy.) Eduardo Frei of the Christian Democratic party, a party that called for widespread social and economic reforms, became president in 1964. He was followed in office

Pinochet (on the podium) led the military junta that replaced President Salvador Allende in 1973. Within a few years, Pinochet had taken over most of the junta's powers, but his rule is scheduled to end in 1990.

by Salvador Allende Gossens, of the Socialist party, who was supported by several left-wing groups. Allende was the first socialist to be elected president in the Western Hemisphere.

Allende's program of changes, which he called the Chilean Road to Socialism, included government control of mining and industry, grants of land to peasants, and redistribution of the country's wealth to the lower classes. He continued to gain support among the poor and the laboring class, but he lost support among middle-class Chileans. When Chile's economy failed to prosper under Allende's government, Pinochet and the army stepped in. In 1973, they installed the military government that ruled Chile for the next 15 years.

Pinochet's government reversed some of the changes that had been made under Allende and also cut back some social programs, such as welfare benefits and medical care for the poor, that had existed for years before Allende came to power. In addition, Chile's human-rights record under Pinochet has been condemned by the United Nations as one of the world's worst. Since 1973, the entire structure of government has been controlled by a handful of military officers who have repeatedly declared nationwide states of emergency or states of siege—in order, they have claimed, to suppress riots or antigovernment violence. According to military experts in other nations, many of these states of emergency or siege have been unnecessary. They have, however, given the government the opportunity to jail its opponents without trial and to limit severely the people's rights to free speech and assembly. A number of books and articles have called the world's attention to the Pinochet government's use of imprisonment, threats, and torture to silence opposing views.

Before 1973, Chile was renowned for its respect for constitutional government and the rule of law. It had also won admiration for the extent and quality of its educational system and health care. These advances have been eroded in recent years, but the Chileans who voted against Pinochet in 1988, as well as friends of Chile around the world, hope that a return to civilian government will renew the spirit of this dynamic, diverse country.

Downtown Santiago spreads out below a cable car running up San Cristobal Hill, part of a city park in the capital. The park features a public zoo, picnic areas, and gardens—a welcome break from the densely populated central city.

A Land of Extremes

In the 1940s, Chilean writer Benjamín Subercaseaux called Chile's geography *loca* (crazy) because it includes so many wildly different kinds of climate and landscape, often separated from one another by natural barriers. The giant Andes Mountains, one of the world's tallest ranges, seal off the country's eastern border; in many places along the border, passes to Argentina are more than 10,000 feet (3,000 meters) above sea level. The smaller *cordillera* (system of mountain ranges) along the western coast isolates the coastline from the rest of the country. The northern third of the country is the Atacama Desert, the world's driest. The center is a region of rich farmland. The southern third is a spectacular but rugged landscape of lakes and volcanoes, which breaks up into a string of cold and rainy islands. With the addition of rain forests, snowfields, beaches, and glaciers, Chile is truly a land of geographic extremes.

It is a long, ribbonlike land that covers the greatest inhabited range of latitude, or north-south distance, of any country in the world. If Chile were placed on top of North America, it would reach from southern Alaska to southern Mexico—a distance of 2,653 miles (4,270 kilometers) from north to south. Yet Chile is only 221 miles (356 kilometers) across from east to west at its widest point, just north of the city of Antofagasta, and 40 miles (64 kilometers) across at its narrowest point. The average width of the country is 109 miles (175 kilometers). Chile is the fourth-largest country in South America (after Brazil, Argentina, and Peru). Its area of 292,257 square miles (756,626 square kilometers) makes it about twice the size of the state of California in the United States, but Chile has only about half as many people as California.

Violent natural forces have shaped Chile's geography. One such force is water. Along the entire length of the Andes, melting snow-fields cause deadly floods that can ruin crops and destroy villages. Another mighty natural force is fire—the fiery power of the volcanoes that dot the country. Many are now extinct, having spent their fire in eruptions of lava ages ago, but a few still simmer and smolder. Countries with mountain ranges and volcanoes often experience earthquakes, and Chile is no exception. Massive, devastating earthquakes originate when the huge plate of the earth's surface that bears the Andes jars against the plate that carries the Chile Rise, an underwater mountain range in the Pacific Ocean. In the past, earthquakes have destroyed cities such as Valparaíso and Concepción; Chileans rebuilt their cities on the ruins. In 1938, a quake killed 50,000 people and worsened the economic chaos of the Great Depression by flattening towns and factories.

Peaks and Valleys

Geographers divide Chile into three parts according to the geographic features that run from north to south in this narrow land. The easternmost of these features is the Cordillera Domeyko of the Andes Mountains, a spine of towering peaks that enters Chile from Peru and Bolivia in the north and runs along its entire length. On the opposite side of the country is the second major geographic feature, a low range of mountains called the coastal cordillera (Cordillera Patagónica), which runs along most of the Pacific Ocean coast. In the central and northern parts of the country, there is a narrow strip of low, flat beach between the ocean and the coastal cordillera. The third geographic feature is the central lowlands, the long, narrow valley that lies between the coastal cordillera and the Andes. In the south, the Andes decrease in height, the country narrows as the South American continent tapers to a point, and these geographic features are compressed into a single mass of peaks and valleys. The coastal cordillera continues offshore, where its peaks appear as hundreds of islands.

The Andes Mountains are the major geographic feature not only of Chile but of all of western South America. In Chile, the peaks of this range reach heights of 16,500 to 19,500 feet (5,000 to 6,000 meters) between the northern border and Santiago. The highest peaks are Llullaillaco at 22,051 feet (6,723 meters) and Ojos del Salado at 22,572 feet (6,772 meters). Ojos del Salado is only 262 feet (79 meters) lower than Aconcagua, the highest mountain in the

Smoke rising from the Villarica volcano, about 400 miles (640 kilometers) south of Santiago, is a reminder of the powerful natural forces that have shaped Chile's dramatic geography.

Western Hemisphere, which lies just across the border in the Argentine Andes, not far from Santiago. South of Santiago, although their elevation decreases, the mountains rise to more than 6,500 feet (1,950 meters) in many places.

The Andes range is the only area of Chile where arctic conditions and extremely cold winter temperatures are found. Temperatures well below the freezing point, combined with deep snow and strong winds, made the Andes passes dangerous for early explorers and soldiers.

The nature of the Andes changes from north to south. The northernmost region, paralleling the arid Atacama Desert, consists of two parallel rows of peaks that enclose wide *altiplanos*, or high, flat plateaus, which are extensions of the altiplanos of Bolivia. This part of the Andes range is sometimes called the Puna de Atacama. In central Chile, the Andes are narrower and are made up mainly of sedimentary rock, formed when wind or water forced grains of sand together, and of lava. In the south, the slow movement of ice glaciers has shaped the mountains during the past 2.5 million years—a process that continues today. This part of Chile contains 7,000 square miles (18,145 square kilometers) of ice fields, more than anywhere else on earth except the North and South poles.

The central lowland is an important mining and agricultural area because it has been filled with deposits of minerals and sedimentary soil carried by rivers flowing down from the Andes. These deposits provide both the fertile soil and the rich mineral ore on which Chile's economy depends.

From North to South

Although geographers can divide Chile into three long, narrow regions from east to west based on its mountainous features, they also can divide it into six sections from north to south based on temperature, climate, and other characteristics. These six sections are usu-

Although rich in copper, the northern region of Antofagasta is poor in rainfall and vegetation. Only the mines, such as this one, draw workers to the inhospitable area.

ally called Norte Grande (Great North), Norte Chico (Little North), the Central Zone, the Frontier, the Lake Country, and the Far South. But Chile also is divided a third way—politically, into 13 administrative divisions called regions, like the states of the United States or the provinces of Canada. Each of Chile's six geographic sections from north to south contains several of these regions.

Norte Grande consists of the regions of Tarapacá (its capital city is Iquique) and Antofagasta (its capital city is also called Antofagasta). The major portion of these two regions is covered by the Atacama Desert, which reaches as far south as the Copiapó River. Arica, Chile's northernmost city, is located in Tarapacá Region. Although Arica lies within the southern tropics, its average annual temperature is surprisingly cool—only 63°F (17°C). This relatively low temperature is caused by the Humboldt Current, also called the Peru Current, a cold stream within the Pacific Ocean that flows northeast from Antarctica along Chile's west coast. This cold offshore current keeps the temperature of northern Chile moderate and also causes hot air coming from the interior of South America to condense into frequent rainfall along the coast.

Because of the current, parts of Norte Grande coast are quite humid; the port city of Iquique has an average humidity of 81 percent. Inland, however, on the far side of the coastal cordillera, the interior of the Atacama is in some places drier than the Sahara Desert. There are places in Norte Grande where no rainfall has ever been known to occur; many scientists believe that these stretches of the Atacama are the world's most arid environment. When storms occur in the high Andes or the springtime sun melts snow on the mountain peaks, streams rush down into this region from the west, but they are absorbed by the Atacama sands before they can reach the sea. Water is piped to the cities from the Andes or carried in large tank trucks. The characteristic landscape is one of hot red sand and wind-carved rock, framed by rugged mountains, with the distant gleam of snow-capped peaks in the east.

The extreme dryness of this thinly populated part of Chile has helped to preserve relics of the past: mud-brick dwellings, irrigation canals, and even mummified bodies from prehistoric Indian civilizations. San Pedro de Atacama, in Antofagasta Region, is a center for archaeological study in the area; this small town also has Chile's oldest church.

In Norte Grande, the central valley between the coastal cordillera and the Andes rises into a series of high plateaus that hold the rich veins of silver, gold, iron, and, especially, copper that account for much of Chile's economic production. Chuquicamata, the world's largest open-pit copper mine, is located in Antofagasta Region. The mine's workers and their families form a city of 25,000 on a remote, windswept plateau. This area also contains large amounts of *caliche*: deposits of sand, salt, and clay that contain sodium nitrate, once the basis of Chile's vast export trade.

South of Norte Grande is Norte Chico, which consists of the regions of Atacama (capital Copiapó) and Coquimbo (capital La Serena). Geographically, this area is one of transition from the extreme desert of the north to the broad, treeless, grassy plains called steppes. Norte Chico is dry, but not as dry as Norte Grande. Like Norte Grande, Norte Chico contains great mineral wealth, mostly iron, silver, and copper. It has been called the Region of 10,000 Mines because of its importance to Chilean mining during the mid-19th century. This area still accounts for 15 to 20 percent of the nation's

Laborers dig irrigation ditches to divert the rivers flowing down from the Andes to farms south of the Atacama Desert.

A mild climate and rich soil make the central valley region the most productive of Chile's agricultural areas. Here, farmers prepare garlic for planting.

total copper production, but it contains only 3 percent of its arable land (land that can be farmed). Coquimbo Region contains a few sizable rivers that make irrigated farming possible, however, and vegetables and fruit are grown here. The port city of Coquimbo also supports a fishing fleet. Coquimbo Region also contains the National Park of Pichasca and three astronomical observatories, which are located high in the Andes, northeast of La Serena.

South of Norte Chico lies the fertile Central Zone of Chile, which consists of the regions of Valparaíso (capital Valparaíso) and El Libertador General Bernardo O'Higgins (capital Rancagua). Sandwiched between these two is a third region made up of the national capital, Santiago, and its surrounding suburbs. About 70 percent of the country's people live in the Central Zone, which contains rich farmland and has a mild climate. Approximately half of all Chileans live within 100 miles (160 kilometers) of Santiago.

Central Chile contains the country's largest and most important cities. Most of them were founded during the Spanish colonial era. They followed a typically Spanish pattern, with a central square or plaza surrounded by low buildings of adobe (a form of sun-dried brick), which deteriorated quickly. Modern development has brought taller buildings, higher population densities, and many businesses. Urban problems include severe housing shortages and insufficient public utilities such as water and electricity.

Viña del Mar, on the coast near the mouth of the Aconcagua River, has beautiful beaches. It has made Valparaíso Region the heart of Chile's tourist industry, although water pollution in the area became a problem in the late 1980s. Just to the south is the city of Valparaíso, the chief port not only of central Chile but also of the entire country. Santiago, with a population of 4,804,200, is one of the world's most strikingly beautiful cities. It lies midway between the coast and the eastern border, at an altitude of 1,800 feet (556 meters) above sea level, framed by the panorama of the high Andes, which stretch as far as the eye can see to the north and south. In the center of the city, taller than any of the modern steel-and-glass skyscrapers that make up the bustling business district, rises the tree-covered Hill of Santa Lucia, crowned by the fort that was built by Pedro de Valdivia and the Spanish *conquistadores*, or conquerors,

Viña del Mar's calm waters, long stretches of beach, numerous restaurants and discos, and a casino have made it a favorite destination for South American vacationers.

in the 16th century. Downtown Santiago has a mix of 16th- and 17th-century colonial buildings, modern office towers, and shopping malls. The main avenue, which is named for Chilean hero Bernardo O'Higgins, is about 330 feet (112 meters) wide and more than 2 miles (3.2 kilometers) long. It is ornamented with gardens, statues, fountains, and public buildings. Santiago attracts many migrant workers from all over Chile's rural provinces, causing the city's population to grow by two percent each year. Many of these transplanted country people and other urban poor cannot afford or find housing, so they live in makeshift shantytowns (large slums made up of shacks).

El Libertador Region is also named for Bernardo O'Higgins, a leader in Chile's fight for independence, who is sometimes called the Father of the Country. Like Valparaíso Region, El Libertador is a productive farming area. It is also the center of livestock raising in Chile and the home of the *huaso*, the traditional Chilean cowboy.

South of the Central Zone lies Maule Region (capital Talca). Like El Libertador, Maule is primarily a farming region; together with Valparaíso and El Libertador regions, it contains nearly all of Chile's irrigated vineyards and produces most of the Chilean wine that is exported. The soil and climate of these regions are ideal for grapevine cultivation, and some Chilean wines are recognized as among the world's finest.

Some people consider Maule part of the Frontier area of Chile; others believe that the Frontier begins south of Maule, in Bío-Bío Region (capital Concepción), along the Bío-Bío River. Settlers have lived here only since the second half of the 19th century. The region is one of rolling hills, rivers and waterfalls, and forests. Farming and forestry dominate the countryside; wheat cultivation and cattle raising do not require irrigation, as rainfall is plentiful. Most agricultural lands were taken from the Indians, who cleared the forests of the

In the middle of Santiago, the green hill behind the church of Santa Lucia provides a panoramic view of the bustling downtown district.

valley floor and the coastal mountains. The Indians overgrazed and overcultivated much of the coastal range, making it useless for modern farmers.

Concepción (population 714,521) is one of Chile's major cities, an industrial center where paper, steel, and textiles are produced. Bío-Bío Region also is noted for its handicrafts. The town of Quinchamali is the center of production of Chile's distinctive black-clay pottery with white decorations.

Also part of Chile's Frontier is Araucania Region (capital Temuco), which is south of Bío-Bío. The region is named for the Araucanian, or Mapuche, Indians, Chile's original inhabitants. Approximately 200,000 of Chile's 250,000 remaining native Indians still live here in circular thatched huts called *rucas* on reservations formed from the *reducciones*, or community settlements, to which they were confined by the government at the end of the 19th century. But although most of Chile's present-day Indians live in this region, other Chileans live here as well; Araucania has a population of about 677,000. Forestry, farming, and cattle raising are the principal economic activities. Tourists who visit the region's six parks and its lakes and hot springs also contribute to the local economy.

In the southern part of Araucania Region, the Frontier gives way to Chile's spectacularly scenic Lake Country. But the heart of the Lake Country is the next region to the south, Los Lagos (capital Puerto Montt). The coastal part of the Lake Country has been compared to Norway and to the Pacific Northwest of North America, with its jagged coastline broken by hundreds of steep, winding fjords, its cool, damp weather, its frequent rains and fogs, and its dense, lush greenery. The interior of the Lake Country, however, is sometimes called the Switzerland of South America. It is a land of pine forests and wildflowers, of clear blue lakes held in basins gouged by glaciers, and of dark, symmetrical, cone-shaped volcanoes whose snow-streaked summits occasionally fume with smoke and steam. Among the largest and most beautiful of the hundreds of lakes are Lake Budi, located in southern Araucania, which is South America's only saltwater lake, and Lakes Ranco and Llanquihue in Los Lagos. Fishing, sight-seeing, and skiing bring many tourists to the Lake Country; tourism, farming, and forestry are the principal economic activities. The Lake Country is Chile's main supplier of oats and potatoes. About half the population of the Lake Country lives in towns or cities, of which the largest are Valdivia, Puerto Montt, and Osorno.

Midway along the coast of Los Lagos Region, the cliffs and hills of the rugged shoreline break up into an archipelago, or string, of thousands of equally rugged islands that trail southward toward the tip of the continent. The largest of these islands, and the only one with a significant number of inhabitants, is Chiloé Island, in Los

Lagos Region. Heavily forested and shrouded in mist, Chiloé was believed by the Indians to be the home of spirits. Chilean writer Ariel Dorfman said of Chiloé in 1985, "Fjords and foggy weather are tempered by rolling hills filled with forests and skies alight with multiple rainbows." He described how the island's 120,000 inhabitants "spend their days tending livestock and fishing, and their nights swapping tales about trolls, phantom pirate ships and-witches."

The portion of Chile that is called the Far South begins at Chiloé Island. It includes the southernmost part of Los Lagos Region and all of Chile's two remaining regions: Aisén del General Carlos Ibáñez del Campo (capital Coihaique) and Magallanes (capital Punta Arenas). Together, these two southern provinces make up almost one-third of Chile's territory, but they contain only three percent of its total population. The Far South is a land of lonely majesty and fierce elements. Cold, strong winds blow year-round, and storms, rough seas, and heavy rainfall plague the coast.

Aisén Region, the country's least populated, is sometimes called Chile's Final Frontier. It is a wilderness of mountains, twisting valleys, glaciers, and damp green pastures and forests. Settlement began in the 1920s, when cattle companies brought ranchers and workers into the area; today sheep ranching is being developed in Aisén. The area has petroleum deposits, and the government hopes to encourage development of these resources in the future.

Magallanes Region is named for Ferdinand Magellan, the explorer who rounded South America from the Atlantic Ocean side, discovered Chile, and claimed it for Spain in 1520. Its coast is a maze of rocky islands and fjords. Inland, the southeastern corner of the country is part of Patagonia—the name given by the Spanish explorers to the plains of southern South America. Stretching from Argentina into Chile, Patagonia is a land of wide horizons and treeless, grass-covered hills. It supports thousands of wild sheep that ranchers gather and shear.

At the southern tip of Chile near Punta Arenas, sheep ranchers watch their herds trot across the Patagonian plains.

Magallanes Region is divided into two parts by a winding waterway called the Strait of Magellan—it was through this passage that Magellan sailed from the Atlantic into the Pacific Ocean. Punta Arenas, the largest city of the Far South and a center of sheep ranching and oil and gas exploration, is located on the northern shore of the strait. Across the strait lies the southern extremity of the Americas, the island called Tierra del Fuego (Land of Fire, named by the Spanish who saw Indian fires burning on its shores). Chile owns the western part of Tierra del Fuego, and Argentina the eastern. The tiny town of Puerto Williams, on the southern shore of Tierra del Fuego, is the farthest south of Chile's settlements. A cluster of barren islets called the Wollaston Islands lies just off Puerto Williams. These islands form the tip of the continent, called Cape Horn. Beyond Cape Horn, the Atlantic and the Pacific oceans meet in the cold waters of the Drake Passage, first navigated by English mariner Francis Drake in 1578, which separates Tierra del Fuego from Antarctica.

Climate and Weather

In keeping with its geographic diversity, Chile has a climate that goes from one extreme in the north to another in the south. The only aspect of the climate that does not change from one end of Chile to the other is the Andean highlands, which are always cold and snowy.

The dry north has a desert climate, where rainfall varies from none in parts of the Atacama Desert to 1 inch (25 millimeters) a year in Copiapó to about 16 inches (400 millimeters) a year in the Aconcagua Valley. Over one 19-year period, the city of Arica recorded a total rainfall of three-hundredths of an inch (three-fourths of a millimeter). The north is hot, although the Humboldt Current keeps it from being as hot as other tropical deserts—La Serena, for example, has an average annual temperature of 57°F (14°C).

Central Chile enjoys a climate like that of the Mediterranean region or central California, with mild, wet winters and long, dry summers. Temperatures here vary hardly at all and are only rarely higher than their January average of 68°F (20°C) or lower than their July average of 50°F (10°C). Santiago's average annual temperature is 57°F (14°C). The heat of summer is seldom oppressive, and frost during the winter is equally rare. Because rainfall in Chile increases from north to south, the center of the country is wetter than the north. Santiago receives an average of 14 inches (355 millimeters) of rain each year, and Concepción gets anywhere from 20 to 40 inches (500 to 1,000 millimeters). Most of central Chile's rain falls during the winter (which in the Southern Hemisphere runs roughly from May through August), so crops must be irrigated in the summer.

South of the Bío-Bío River, however, rain falls year-round, reaching annual totals of 107 inches (2,707 millimeters) in Valdivia and 216 inches (5,379 millimeters) in parts of the Far South. Rainfall here is as heavy as that of any area in the world outside the tropical rain forests. This region is also Chile's coldest. Temperatures range from Valdivia's annual average of 53°F (11.5°C) to Punta Arenas's annual average of 43°F (6°C). Tierra del Fuego is about as far from the South Pole as Alaska is from the North Pole, yet the island's weather is much milder than than that of its northern counterpart. It seldom experiences weather colder than 21°F (-6°C), because the moisture produced by the mingling of Atlantic and Pacific Ocean currents keeps the temperatures from becoming bitterly cold.

Plant and Animal Life

Like its geography and its rainfall, Chile's plant life varies greatly from north to south. In the north, the coast and the central valley are almost completely barren—this area is the closest approach to an absolute desert, void of all life, to be found anywhere on earth. Closer to the Andes, however, where a bit of moisture from storms and melting snow reaches the Atacama sands, the cover of vegetation is thicker. A form of hardy desert brush called tola grows there, as do many varieties of cactus, small shrubs, and plants with spiny thorns. Grasses appear on the lower slopes of the Andes foothills.

In addition to the great variety of cultivated plants, central Chile's vegetation includes plains of rather poor grass, dotted with cactus and espino shrubs; many of the shrubs have disappeared because rural workers have uprooted them to make fires. The red, bell-shaped copihue, Chile's national flower, is found throughout this area of Mediterranean climate.

Grass grows more lushly near the Bío-Bío River, and south of the river much of the land is covered with dense forests that provide an important source of timber. These forests contain both deciduous trees (trees that lose their leaves each year), such as beeches, and evergreens (trees that keep their leaves year-round), such as laurels. Other tree species found in southern Chile include the magnolia, several kinds of pine, the tall and stately araucaria (also found in Australia), and valuable hardwoods such as alamo, lenga, and olivillo, which are used in making furniture. The monkey puzzle tree, native to this part of Chile, has been carried to the United States and Europe, where it is used as an ornamental tree. True rain forests are found in parts of the Lake Country, especially along the ocean coast near Valdivia. Here vines, shrubs, ferns, mosses, pine trees, and wild bamboo form impassable thickets.

The trees grow smaller and more stunted south of Chiloé Island, and much of the Far South is too cold and windy to support heavy forests. Small pines and shrubs, bent by the ceaseless force of the wind, cover the landscape, giving way to treeless grasslands in Patagonia and Tierra del Fuego.

Animal life in Chile lacks the variety of other South American nations, mostly because the barrier of the Andes Mountains has kept many species from migrating into Chile. Farm animals, such as cattle, sheep, and goats, were imported by settlers and are found throughout the central and southern parts of the country.

Native wildlife in the dry northern plateaus includes several long-necked members of the camel family: the llama, the alpaca, and the vicuña. All of these have dense, silky fleece that provides high-quality wool; that of the vicuña is considered the finest. A fourth camel relative, the guanaco, once flourished in Chile but has been hunted to near extinction. The northern mountains are home to the Andean wolf, to the large cat that is called both puma and cougar, to the Andean condor (the largest bird of the Western Hemisphere), and to a deer called the guemul. Both the Andean condor and the guemul appear on the Chilean coat of arms, but both are becoming disturbingly rare, and the guemul has been placed on the endangered-species list. Other endangered species in Chile are the tundra peregrine falcon, the Chilean wood star (a small bird), and

the puna rhea (an ostrichlike, flightless bird of the high altiplano). The chinchilla, a rodent with extremely valuable fur, has been hunted so much that it is virtually extinct in the wild.

The wildlife of the southern forests includes the chilla (similar to a fox), several kinds of marsupials, such as opossums, and the spike-horned pudu, the world's smallest deer. The Chilean bullfrog, whose booming call is one of the background noises of the forest, is prized as a delicacy by the local inhabitants. Only a few species of freshwater fish are native to Chile's lakes and streams, but North American trout have been introduced successfully into the Lake Country, where the trout fishing is among the world's best. The wet and stormy southern regions are inhospitable by land, but the off-

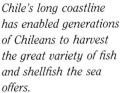

Chile's long coastline has enabled generations of Chileans to harvest the great variety of fish and shellfish the sea offers.

shore waters are filled with fish, which provide food for whales, six species of seals, several species of penguins, and dozens of other kinds of water birds.

Chile's Territories

In addition to the mainland and the offshore islands, Chile owns six Pacific island territories. Nearest to the mainland is the cluster called the Diego Ramírez Islands, about 60 miles (100 kilometers) southwest of Cape Horn. This handful of rocky islets is uninhabited.

About 360 miles (580 kilometers) west of Valparaíso lie a group of volcanic, tree-covered islands called the Juan Fernández Islands. They were discovered by navigator Juan Fernández sometime before

1572, but they did not become well known until a mariner named Alexander Selkirk was shipwrecked on one of the islands in 1704 and remained there until he was rescued in 1709. His adventure is generally believed to be the basis for Daniel Defoe's novel *Robinson Crusoe*. Today, the two largest islands of the group are called Robinson Crusoe and Alejandro Selkirk. The islands' several hundred inhabitants support themselves by lobster fishing.

Two tiny island territories, San Ambrosio and San Félix, were discovered in 1574. San Ambrosio lies 600 miles (965 kilometers) west of Chile, and San Félix is 12 miles (19 kilometers) southwest of San Ambrosio. Both are dry, desolate, and uninhabited.

Also uninhabited is Sala y Gomez Island, located 2,100 miles (3,380 kilometers) west of the mainland. It is only 4,000 feet (1,200 meters) long and 500 feet (150 meters) wide.

About 250 miles (400 kilometers) southwest of Sala y Gomez lies Chile's most famous territory, Easter Island (called Isla de Pascua in Spanish and Rapa-Nui in Polynesian). It lies 2,300 miles (3,700 kilometers) from the mainland and is 15 miles (24 kilometers) long and 10 miles (16 kilometers) wide. Easter Island is actually the peak of a submerged volcano, now no longer active.

Although Easter Island was discovered by the English buccaneer Edward Davis in the 1680s, it was the Dutch navigator Jacob Roggeveen who gave it its name when he landed there on Easter Sunday in 1722. The island was claimed by Spain in 1770 and taken over by Chile in 1888. It is now administered as part of Valparaíso Region. Nearly one-third of the island consists of a national park, designed to attract tourists to this remote Pacific outpost.

At the time of its discovery, Easter Island was inhabited by several thousand Polynesian people, whose language and customs were related to those of the inhabitants of Tahiti and other Pacific islands to the west. Scholars believe that these early Polynesians

made their way eastward across the Pacific in large canoes, coloniz-
ing new islands as they came. Easter Island was the easternmost
point they reached. Today, about 500 of their descendants remain
on Easter Island, which is also inhabited by about 1,500 people from
mainland Chile. The people are farmers, raising sugarcane, yams,
bananas, and potatoes.

Easter Island's fame rests on the hundreds of massive carved
stone heads, called *moais*, that have been found lying or standing
all over the island. The heads are made of a dark volcanic stone
called tufa and are of all sizes; the largest are more than 90 feet (30
meters) tall and weigh more than 200 tons. Archaeologists (scientists
who study the remains of earlier human cultures) are still unraveling
the mysteries of the statues' origins and meaning.

Chile also claims part of Antarctica—a wedge-shaped area of
483,000 square miles (1,250,000 square kilometers) across the Drake
Passage from Cape Horn that includes the Antarctic Peninsula (called
the O'Higgins Peninsula in Chile). Parts of this area, however, are
also claimed by Argentina and the United Kingdom. For the present,
an international treaty forbids enforcement of territorial claims in
Antarctica, although conflict over such claims could arise if the
treaty is not renewed in the 1990s.

The proud Araucanians, or Mapuche, the original inhabitants of Chile, resisted Spanish conquest for 350 years. Approximately 250,000 pure-blooded Mapuche remain, more than four-fifths of them on reservations in Araucania Region.

Early History and Conquest

When the Spanish first explored Chile in 1536, between 500,000 and 1,000,000 Indians lived within the country's present borders. Archaeologists believe that these Indians first emerged as a people about 10,000 years ago, when nomadic (traveling) tribes journeyed down through the valleys of the Andes into Chile. These various tribes were later given the name Araucanians by the Spanish. The Araucanians of northern and central Chile called themselves the Picunche; those of the Frontier area in south-central Chile were the Mapuche; and those of the Far South were the Huilliche. The largest group of the Araucanians was the Mapuche, and today the terms *Mapuche* and *Araucanian* are used interchangeably to refer to Chile's native Indians.

By the early 1400s, the Araucanians of northern Chile were ruled and influenced by the powerful Inca civilization of Peru and Bolivia. But the difficulties of land travel in Chile, together with the harsh climate of many regions, discouraged the development of an advanced civilization such as that of the Incas. The Picunche in the north hunted and gathered food from the wild; they also raised llamas and farmed near the region's few springs and streams. In the productive central part of the country, most Picunche and Mapuche lived in villages, where the major activities were hunting and farming. In the cold Far South, hunting and fishing were the Huilliche's primary means of survival.

Early Explorations

Although Magellan's ships sailed up part of the Chilean coast in 1520, the Spanish were the true explorers of Chile. Diego de Almagro, the first Spanish adventurer in Chile, was one of the lieutenants of Francisco Pizarro, the Spanish conquistador, or conqueror, who overthrew the wealthy Inca Empire of Peru in 1532. The conquerors of Peru won an almost unimaginably huge treasure in gold and silver, but they wanted still more. Eager to rid their land of as many Spanish as possible, the Incas told the conquistadores that the countries to the south held even more gold and silver. So, in 1536, Almagro led an expedition of about 600 men south in search of "otro Perú" (another Peru). He spent a year and a half crossing the high altiplano and the Andes Mountains, only to find the world's driest desert and its inhabitants, warlike Indians who produced only enough food for their own survival. Of gold and silver there was no sign. Almagro then returned to Peru to fight Pizarro for control of Cuzco, then the capital of Peru. After Almagro was captured in battle, Pizarro's brother had him executed.

In 1540, a conquistador named Pedro de Valdivia invested the fortune he had accumulated in Peru in a second expedition into Chile. The journey attracted only about 150 Spanish adventurers, although, like Almagro's, it was accompanied by several thousand Indians carrying supplies. Valdivia was also accompanied by his mistress, Ines de Suárez, who proved to be a courageous and resourceful partner in the adventures that lay ahead. They arrived in Chile in 1541, and Valdivia claimed the land as a colony of Spain. He founded Santiago in February and appointed a *cabildo* (council) of conquis-

Diego de Almagro was the first Spanish conquistador to visit Chile, in 1536. Instead of gold and silver, he found fierce Indians.

tadores to control local affairs. He also distributed *encomiendas,* or "trusteeships," to his followers. As trustees, the Spanish could control large estates and collect tribute, or taxes, from the Indians in return for introducing the Indians to Christianity. But the Indians had very little gold and silver and so could pay meager tribute. As a result, even though the Spanish king had made laws against enslaving the Indians for any reason, many ended up as badly off as slaves, paying their tribute in the form of forced labor on the conquistadores' estates. Men, women, and children, old and young alike, worked at farming, mining, and carrying heavy loads of provisions during military campaigns, an activity that killed them by the thousands.

During the next decade, Valdivia pushed south from Santiago into the area that is still called the Frontier because it was the site of many battles with the Indians. Valdivia set up forts and small settlements, including Concepción. Although today it is one of Chile's largest cities, Concepción was destroyed many times by attackers, earthquakes, and tidal waves during the colonial period.

In December 1553, Valdivia, then in Concepción, learned that three Spanish men had been murdered by Indians near the fort at Tucapel. Angry and determined to avenge the soldiers' deaths, Valdivia took 40 of his best fighters and set out for the fort. He arrived on Christmas morning to find the fort entirely destroyed.

As he climbed the last small hill toward the fort, Valdivia did not know that an army of Indians lay waiting for him, led by his former Indian stableboy, Lautaro, who had escaped from his service. Suddenly a small band of Indian warriors came charging at the soldiers. Spanish guns fired, and many of the Indians were wounded or killed. But another band came, and another, until finally the Spanish who remained alive decided to retreat. But they could not outrun the Indians, and all were captured.

No one really knows what happened to Pedro de Valdivia. Indian legend says that Lautaro's men killed Valdivia by pouring molten gold—the metal so earnestly sought by the Spanish—down his throat. But it is more likely that after his capture Valdivia was executed by having his head cut off.

Pedro de Valdivia, along with his mistress Inez de Suárez, founded Santiago on February 12, 1541. He continued to push southward and founded the city of Concepción, but he was killed by Indians intent on driving the Spanish from their land.

Colonial History and Independence

Despite setbacks such as Valdivia's death and continued Indian resistance, the Spanish eventually dominated much of Chile, and Spanish colonists began to settle there. During the colonial period, Chile was known as a captaincy general of Spain and was supposed to be administered from the viceroyalty of Peru. In theory, Chile's captain general, or governor, was subject to the authority of the king of Spain and also to the viceroy of Peru. But in practice, because Chile was so difficult to reach, local affairs were mostly controlled by the governor, who commanded the army, and by the cabildo of each town. Neither the king nor the Roman Catholic church was much interested in Chile, as it was so much poorer than Mexico and Peru in gold and silver. Very few competent church or government officials came to Chile except in the hope of being promoted to service in the wealthier colonies.

Besides its lack of wealth, Chile suffered from constant war. Starting around 1600, the colonists made renewed attempts to push southward from the central district, only to meet unyielding resistance from the Mapuche. From this time through the mid-1700s, the burden of financing the "perpetual war" against the Indians was shifted to Peru, which provided Chile with money to maintain a government in Santiago and an army on the frontier. This *situado*, as the subsidy of money was called, became a lasting symbol of Chile's poverty and dependence.

Indian victories during the 1620s and 1630s led to the signing of a truce called the Pact of Quillon in 1646—the only pact in all of Spanish America that recognized Indian control over territory. It said that if the Indians would return their Spanish captives and allow missionaries to spread Christianity, the Spanish would remain north of the Bío-Bío River. But the Indians broke the truce, the war continued, and the Spanish settled south of the Bío-Bío. Just when the Spanish thought they controlled the Bío-Bío Valley, in 1655, Indians destroyed all Spanish settlements there, including Concepción. The Spanish rebuilt their settlements and continued to push southward.

Around 1700, the Spanish throne passed from the Hapsburg family to the Bourbon family. The Bourbons made changes, called the "Bourbon reforms," in certain colonial policies. These reforms gave Chilean colonists the right to exchange goods directly with European nations instead of sending their trade through Peru. Trade at once became quicker and less costly. Another reform was the banishing from Spanish America in 1767 of the Jesuit religious order, whose missionaries had angered the colonists by protecting the Indians, converting them to Christianity, organizing them into religious villages, and preserving them from enslavement. Once the Jesuits were forced out, new immigrants from Europe were happy to take over land that had once belonged to the missionaries, but the absence of the Jesuits meant a lack of skilled teachers. Chilean education remained two centuries behind that of Mexico and Peru until the Jesuits returned in the mid-19th century.

For the most part, other than the constant Indian wars in the south, Chile was a quiet colonial backwater for several centuries. Over time, however, a new class developed: the Creoles. These were people who had been born and raised in Chile, as opposed to the Spanish who came to Chile to work but planned to return to Spain someday. The Creoles were committed to Chilean lives for themselves and their children. Many of them felt little loyalty to far-off Spain, and they began to claim that Chile would be better off with more self-government, lower taxes, and less interference from its Spanish overlords.

The French emperor Napoleon Bonaparte conquered Spain in 1808 and installed his brother as the new Spanish king. The disorder in Spain encouraged many Spanish colonies to seek self-rule. In Chile in 1810, a *cabildo abierto* (open town meeting) elected a junta, or ruling committee, of local leaders to replace the Spanish governor. The leader of the junta, José Miguel Carrera, wanted complete independence from Spain. But some members of the wealthier classes, hoping to preserve their status, felt that the new government should not go so far. Before this disagreement was settled, Spanish troops defeated the rebellious Chileans at the Battle of Rancagua in 1814 and regained control of Chile.

Bernardo O'Higgins was one of many Chilean rebels who fled to Argentina after the defeat at Rancagua. He was the illegitimate son of an Irish soldier of fortune named Ambrosio O'Higgins, who had become the viceroy of Peru. In Argentina he became acquainted with José de San Martín, the military leader who had recently liberated Argentina from Spain. With O'Higgins's help, San Martín devised a plan to reclaim Chile and to conquer Peru, the center of

José de San Martín and Bernardo O'Higgins celebrate the liberation of Chile from the Spanish.

Spanish authority in South America. After a difficult journey through mountain passes that earned San Martín the name Knight of the Andes, the rebel army defeated the Spanish in 1817 outside Santiago. Within the year, O'Higgins was appointed supreme dictator of the newly independent nation of Chile.

Spanish Treatment of the Indians

The Araucanians did not submit to the Spanish without a long, bitter fight. The Picunche of the north, who were accustomed to domination by the Incas, were quickly controlled and became laborers for the Spanish. But the Mapuche, and to a lesser extent the Huilliche, continued to fight against Spanish control for 350 years, through the 1880s.

The Mapuche were among the few Indians in the Americas to resist the Spanish successfully. Lautaro, the escaped slave who led the battle against Valdivia, was a Mapuche. Today he is regarded as the national hero of Chile's Indians. His exploits and the bravery of the Mapuche were celebrated in a long epic poem called *La Araucana* (The Araucanian), written in the late 1500s by a Spanish soldier named Alonso de Ercilla y Zúñiga, who had come from Spain to fight the Indians.

The frozen remains of a young Indian princess were perfectly preserved in the icy heights of the Andes Mountains for almost 500 years. From such finds, anthropologists hope to learn more about Indian culture before the Spanish arrived.

The Araucanians won many battles because of their ability to change their weapons and fighting style to suit the circumstances. They learned to ride horses by copying the Spanish (horses did not exist in the Americas until the Spanish brought them), and they also scavenged broken bits of Spanish swords to make sharp, deadly arrowheads. The Indians destroyed Spanish settlements, waiting for harvest season so they could ruin the Spanish crops, as the Spanish had ruined theirs. After allowing the Spanish to rebuild, the Indians destroyed the settlements all over again.

But the Spanish took revenge, although Spain officially prohibited mistreatment of the Indians. During the 1670s, the Jesuit missionaries won the king's permission to free Christian Indian war prisoners and their children. But both Spanish law and Roman Catholic doctrine permitted enslavement of Indians who refused to be converted to Christianity. Many of the Indians who were captured in battles thus became slaves to fill the needs of Spanish landowners. Those who failed to obey were subject to dreadful cruelty: They were blinded or had their hands, feet, noses, or ears cut off. One early colonial governor of the 1500s went so far as to order Indian prisoners' feet mutilated to prevent escape, then had the slaves' feet dipped in boiling fat to keep the Indians from dying of blood loss. Spanish troops sometimes trapped Indian families inside their houses, then set the buildings on fire. They raped Indian women, and as a form of entertainment they watched while prisoners in chains were torn to pieces by dogs. As in nearly all of North and South America, the suppression and exploitation of native peoples by Europeans was a shameful chapter in history. No wonder an Araucanian chief said, "The King is good and he legislates justly, but your governors and captains do not comply and there is no justice for the Indians."

The Chamber of Deputies, the lower house of Congress, was for 150 years the scene of hard-fought power struggles between the Liberal and Conservative parties and between the president and Congress. Pinochet dissolved Congress for the first time in the history of independent Chile in 1973.

Modern History to 1964

From 1818 to 1823, Chile was ruled by its first leader, dictator Bernardo O'Higgins, who built a navy, opened schools and libraries, and enacted laws to promote trade and agriculture. In the mid-1820s, two parties emerged to dominate Chilean political life. The Conservatives (known as *pelucones*, or "bigwigs") were mostly landowners and church officials. They preferred a strong central government and a president who would look after their interests. The Liberals (known as *pipiolos*, or "novices") favored a strict constitutional form of government, redistribution of land from the big estate holders to the smaller farmers and peasants, and limits on the power of the Catholic church. The conflict between these points of view has shaped Chilean politics to the present day.

A civil war in 1830 left the Conservatives in power. From 1831 through 1861, three Conservative presidents served two terms each. But Diego Portales, a tobacco merchant who became a government minister, ruled the country from behind the scenes as a virtual dictator until 1837. A man who said that he would shoot his own father if it were necessary to maintain public order, Portales believed that Chile had fallen into "bad habits" of banditry, political disturbances, and freedom of the press.

Portales also said that "the weight of the night . . . the masses' near universal tendency to repose was the guarantee of public tranquility," meaning that he believed the population in general was ignorant, resistant to change, and uninterested in fighting for unpopular beliefs. (At this time, Chile's lower classes of poor and laboring people were called the *rotos*, or "broken ones.") But if any of the slumbering masses happened to wake up and speak out, Portales used fear and repression to make sure they were not heard.

The constitution of 1833, which remained in force through 1925, contained many of Portales's ideas. Under this constitution, the president held most of the power, control over local affairs rested with the central government, and Roman Catholicism was made the state religion, with priests' salaries paid by the government. Furthermore, the constitution limited voting rights to men who owned land or could read, which meant that an oligarchy (a small group of wealthy or privileged individuals) could control elections.

Chilean education improved during the 1840s. New educational institutions were founded, including the University of Chile in Santiago. A number of writers, scholars, and philosophers from Chile and other Spanish-American countries formed a group called the Generation of 1842 after the year of the university's founding. This group urged, through articles in newspapers and magazines, that Chile enact social and political reforms and train teachers for the future. Members of the Generation of 1842 gave new life to the old Liberal party, which gained support during the 1850s and came to dominate the government from 1861 to 1891. The Liberals fought against censorship of the press, excessive presidential power, and restrictions on voting rights.

Many changes in Chile's economy took place during the 19th century, although economic progress was limited. Railways and telegraph lines spread throughout the country, carrying both goods and news, and the invention of the steamship increased trade with

Shots were exchanged in Valparaíso harbor during an unsuccessful uprising against Conservative party rule in 1851. The Liberals came to power peacefully in 1861.

other nations. More and more people moved to the cities. Copper and silver exports became crucial to the Chilean economy. Yet during the 50 years after independence, neither the landowners nor the mine operators introduced modern machinery. Instead of investing in expensive equipment, they relied on the labor of a large number of *inquilinos* (workers bound to their employers by debt). Because the inquilinos could be made to work for very low wages, the employers accumulated large profits. Landowners also did not plant crops on all the land they owned, because by not producing too much, they could guarantee high prices for their produce. With up-to-date equipment and full use of the land, Chile's agricultural production could have been much greater than it was, and modernization of the mining industry would have allowed much more of the refining work to take place inside the country, thus providing jobs for Chileans. Instead, Chile shipped its raw ores to be refined elsewhere. The country developed almost no manufacturing industries and relied on natural resources alone for economic growth.

The sheltered harbor of Valparaíso has always been Chile's busiest port. The invention of the steamship in the 1800s made the harbor even more important as Chile's economy began to depend increasingly on exports of raw materials.

By the 1870s, many Chilean workers had traveled north to Bolivia and Peru to work in the nitrate mines and refineries of the Atacama Desert, which belonged to those two nations. Other Chileans found work in the Atacama on construction crews building railroads to link the mines of the interior with the coastal ports. Chile and Bolivia had agreed to share the profits from nitrate production and exports, but Bolivia did not pay Chile its share of the export fees it collected from nations that bought the nitrates. Then Bolivia announced that it would raise taxes against Chilean companies that helped operate the mines. In 1879, the Chilean firms refused to pay the taxes. Bolivia promptly seized Chilean-owned nitrate plants in the Antofagasta area, which was then Bolivian territory, and threatened to auction them off to pay the taxes. Chile responded by sending its army into the area. Bolivia then declared war upon Chile, as did Peru, honoring a secret defense pact with Bolivia.

The following conflict, known as the War of the Pacific, lasted from 1879 to 1883. At its end, the victorious Chilean army had occupied Lima, Peru's capital, and Chile obtained a valuable parcel of territory in the north that increased its size by more than one-third. Arica, which had belonged to Peru, and Antofagasta, which had belonged to Bolivia, were now part of Chile. The results of the war were especially unfortunate for Bolivia, which lost not only its nitrate fields but also its only access to the Pacific. To this day, landlocked Bolivia lays claim to a strip of land in Chile leading to the sea, but Chile is unlikely ever to honor this claim.

Balmaceda and the Constitutional Crisis

A strange and tragic episode in Chilean history was the presidency of José Manuel Balmaceda, who took office in 1886, not long after Chile won the War of the Pacific. At this time, the government had placed high taxes on exports of nitrates—the more nitrate produced, the more money the government collected. Balmaceda wanted to use this money for an ambitious program of public works, such as extending the railroad and telegraph systems and building more schools.

During this period, privately owned companies controlled both the nitrate production and the railroads that linked the nitrate mines with the port cities. If the price of nitrate on the world markets fell, the heads of the companies would meet and decide to reduce the total amount of nitrate produced, thus making nitrate more scarce and raising its price. (Such practices, known as price-fixing, are today illegal in many countries.) These cutbacks in nitrate production both eliminated jobs and reduced the government's income from export taxes. For these reasons, Balmaceda wanted to wrest some control of the nitrate industry away from the handful of powerful companies that ran it.

At the same time, however, Balmaceda angered legislators by appointing cabinet ministers without regard to the wishes of Congress, by refusing to call the Congress into session when requested to do so, and by failing to accept Congress's decision that a number of ministers must resign. This was completely unexpected, because when Balmaceda was a member of Congress he had fought to preserve its power against a series of strong presidents. In addition, Balmaceda was attempting to force Congress to approve his nomination for president in 1891, at which time his own term would end under the constitution. Congress passed a law that made the nomination illegal. Balmaceda refused to sign it, and tension between the president and Congress increased.

In early 1891, Balmaceda illegally decreed that the government would continue to spend money despite Congress's orders that it must approve all spending. Congress gained control of the navy and ordered it to sail to the far north and seize the nitrate taxes so that Balmaceda could not spend them. Meanwhile, Balmaceda announced

Chile acquired the nitrate fields of Peru and Bolivia after winning the War of the Pacific, but the mines themselves, although they provided jobs and tax revenues for Chileans, were mostly owned by British investors.

The harbor of Antofagasta was Bolivia's only outlet to the sea. Chile seized it after the War of the Pacific, gaining a convenient port for nitrate exports and making Bolivia a landlocked nation.

a state of siege, suspended civil liberties and freedom of the press, and used the army in an attempt to put down the rebellious Congress and the navy. Civil war broke out.

In the end, Balmaceda lost. Because there was no railway between Santiago and the far north—Balmaceda had hoped to build one as part of his public works program—the president's army could not reach the Atacama area, much less engage the navy in battle. The navy seized the nitrate taxes and used the money to buy equipment for the war. Congress raised its own army, which was commanded by Emil Korner, a former Prussian officer who had been hired by Balmaceda many years before to modernize Chile's armed forces. The bloody civil war lasted about 7 months; 10,000 men lost their lives.

Balmaceda, however, remained in Chile through the final day of his term as president. On that day, September 18, 1891, he wrote letters to members of his family and his closest friends, as well as a statement in which he tried to explain and justify his actions. The next morning, the former president rose early. Dressed entirely in black, he put a revolver to his head and shot himself.

Political and Social Changes to 1939

After the civil war of 1891, the Chilean Congress became much stronger. Many congressmen were from the upper classes, and therefore wealthy merchants and bankers expected that they, rather than the president, would now decide who served in government and what laws were passed. But there arose a number of parties that favored the interests of the middle and lower classes. Throughout the first two decades of the 20th century, workers in the nitrate industry, the factories, and the public utility industries (railroad, gas, and electricity) often struck in the hope of obtaining better wages and working conditions.

Along with this social unrest, Chile faced economic difficulties. Winning the rich nitrate fields from Peru and Bolivia had allowed the country to postpone the process of modernizing agriculture and building new factories for another 40 years. In addition, most of Chile's arable land was owned by a few wealthy farmers, and under their control the nation produced just enough food to feed itself. Then, during the early 1900s, the government found that it had to obtain loans to repay old debts and cover the expenses of running the country.

During World War I (1914–18), Chile remained neutral. A large population of German immigrants had settled in southern Chile in the years from 1800 to 1850, and their descendants formed a substantial German-Chilean community that favored Germany's position in the war. Most of Chile's trade at the time was with Great Britain, however, and Chile did not want to take the side of Germany

(continued on p. 73)

Scenes of

CHILE

▲ The harsh climate and landscape of southern Chile isolated its inhabitants and discouraged settlement for years. Change comes slowly to this region, and horse-drawn carts still deliver milk on the streets of Punta Arenas (above) and carry businessmen in Puerto Montt (lower right). ➤

◄ A market in Puerto Montt features fruits and vegetables, perhaps from Chile's fertile Central Zone, which ships fresh produce throughout the country's 2,600-mile (4,200-kilometer) length.

↑ *In Magallanes, the farthest south of Chile's provinces, Wards Glacier in Torres del Paine National Park reminds visitors how close to the South Pole they are.*

⋏ *Llamas graze in Lauca National Park in Tarapacá, the northernmost and most arid of Chile's regions. Despite the harsh climate, herds of wild vicuñas also roam the park's desolate reaches.*

▼ *The climate in the extreme south is as severe as in the extreme north. The spectacular Admiralty Fjord on the island of Tierra del Fuego winds its way through steep cliffs cloaked with ice and snow.*

▲ Only 30 miles north of the sophisticated resort city of Viña del Mar, in the small town of Zapallar, Chileans spend Saturday night at the movies.

◄ Thousands of Chileans live crowded into shantytowns in Santiago. Many have left the countryside to seek work in the city but can find work only as street vendors.

▲ *Chile's 33 regional and national parks provide many opportunities for outdoor recreation.*

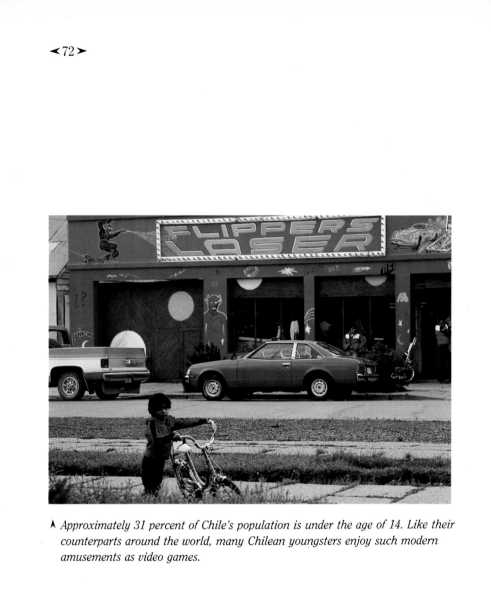

▲ *Approximately 31 percent of Chile's population is under the age of 14. Like their counterparts around the world, many Chilean youngsters enjoy such modern amusements as video games.*

(continued from p. 64)

against its trade partner. As the war cut off access to Great Britain, Chile's trade with the United States increased, particularly in the nitrates that were used to make gunpowder and explosives.

As Chile entered the 1920s, it was consuming more than it produced. When the consumption of goods is high but the supply of those goods is limited, the result is price inflation, or rising costs for goods and services. Rising prices created financial hardship, especially for the middle and lower classes, and led to a decade marked by political turmoil and widespread strikes. The military, which had stayed out of politics for many years, was convinced that incompetent and corrupt politicians were the source of Chile's economic woes. Military leaders seized power twice during the 1920s and tried to encourage economic growth.

The second time the military seized power, it installed Arturo Alessandri Palma, a former president and respected reformer, as president. In October 1925, Alessandri presented the people with a new constitution. This new constitution separated church and state (meaning that the Roman Catholic church was no longer the official state church and that priests would no longer be paid by the government); it made education compulsory (required for all citizens by law); it protected freedom of the press; and it gave voting rights to all male citizens 18 years of age and older. The constitution was approved, but Congress forced Alessandri to resign that same month. A military leader named Carlos Ibáñez del Campo took his place as head of the government, and the constitution was suspended.

By the early 1930s, Chile was in a state of economic misery as a result of the worldwide Great Depression, which caused copper and nitrate prices to fall dramatically. Financial problems caused more political turmoil, which continued until constitutional government was restored in 1932 and Alessandri was reelected. In 1939, the Chilean Development Corporation (CORFO) was established to encourage industrialization.

World War II and After

World War II (1939–45) brought tension to Chile. The United States feared that Chile would favor Hitler's Nazi Germany because of the large number of German-Chileans in southern Chile. At the same time, many Jews and others fleeing Nazi persecution found refuge in Chile. President Juan Antonio Ríos at first agreed with Argentina not to support the anti-German program led by the United States. Later, in 1944, Chile entered the war on the side of the Allies, who included Great Britain and the United States, Chile's chief trade partners. The chief event of the war years in Chile, however, was a devastating earthquake that killed 50,000 people.

Between the early 1930s and the early 1960s, Chile gained a reputation as a bright spot of democratic government in Latin America; this was somewhat unusual in a region where governments are often controlled by powerful individuals, usually military officers. In Chile, the military did not intervene directly in politics during these years. Elections were held on schedule, votes were counted fairly, and a vigorous free press developed and exercised its right to be critical of the government.

In the 1930s, many Chileans who were unsatisfied with economic and political conditions formed new political parties. Chile's large German population contained a small number of Nazis who attempted but failed to overthrow the government in 1938. Here, police arrest the Nazi plotters in Santiago.

Education and culture developed rapidly during these three decades. Catholic schools as well as private, nonreligious ones were founded. National universities started research programs in science, literature, and history. The study of the humanities (subjects such as literature and philosophy) and of social sciences (subjects such as economics and political science) were aided by exchanges of scholars with the United States and the nations of Western Europe. Although this growth helped make Chileans among the most educated people in Latin America, it also created a class of highly trained people for whom the Chilean economy could not yet provide technical or professional jobs. Many of these individuals left Chile for opportunities in other countries.

Other important shifts in Chilean society occurred. Whereas well-educated Chileans left their homeland in search of work, many poor farmers and rural peasants came to the cities looking for jobs. But because there was no work for them, the number of urban poor grew. The number of eligible voters also grew, from 500,000 in 1938 to 2,500,000 in 1963. Women, who had always been more independent in Chile than in other Latin American countries, gained voting rights in 1949. The Communist party was formed in 1921 (but was outlawed from 1948 to 1958); the Socialist party, in 1931; and a moderate political party called the Christian Democrats, in 1957. A severe earthquake in 1960, and the tidal wave that immediately followed, caused widespread destruction and brought economic chaos. By the early 1960s, the government was in the hands of a coalition, or cooperative party, that included both the old Conservative and Liberal parties—but Chileans were restless, and the stage was set for political change.

Salvador Allende was a founder of the Socialist party in Chile in 1933, a member of Congress from 1937 to 1970, and president from 1970 to 1973. His family had long been active in Chilean politics: His great-grandfather fought for Chilean independence under José de San Martín, and his grandfather was one of the leading reformers in 19th-century Chile.

Frei, Allende, and Pinochet

As the 1964 elections approached, the traditional Liberal and Conservative parties lost ground to the relatively new Christian Democratic Party (PDC) and to the coalition of Socialist and Communist parties. On election day, a majority of Chilean voters, discontented with the political and economic stagnation of the past 30 years, elected the PDC candidate, Eduardo Frei.

Frei began to implement a program he called a Revolution in Liberty and proposed a process of "Chileanization," in which copper mines owned by foreign companies would gradually be bought by the government. He also backed an amendment to the constitution that would allow the government to take over parts of large estates that were not being well used and make them available to poor farmers. Groups that had had little power before, including workers, peasants, women, and poor people, became more politically active.

The programs of the Frei government also ensured that by 1973 Chile's educational system was the best Latin America had to offer. Enrollment in primary schools increased even in rural areas. The university system was expanded, and greater emphasis was placed on the study of Chilean history and on training students to solve the problems of economic development that had long confronted Chile. Money was set aside to build schools and increase teachers' salaries.

But the government's goals were too ambitious, especially in the area of economic policy. During the last years of Frei's administration, which ended in 1970, the wealthy and conservative right-wing elements of the population criticized his reforms; the left-wing elements claimed that the reforms had not gone far enough or fast enough. The rate of inflation increased, the economy stagnated, and shortages of consumer goods occurred.

During Frei's term, many Chilean voters, especially the working classes, the poor, and students, moved further to the left—that is, they favored more government action to bring about social and economic change. In 1970, these voters elected Salvador Allende, who was sponsored by the Socialist and Communist parties, to the presidency. The PDC also agreed to support Allende, who in return promised to honor all the provisions of the constitution in governing the land. It was the first free election of a Marxist (that is, someone influenced by the socialist and communist theories of Karl Marx) to a presidency in the Western Hemisphere.

Cheering crowds greeted President Eduardo Frei (center) on his return from a trip to Europe. The people's enthusiasm turned to discontent as Frei's economic policies failed to satisfy their expectations.

Chilean Socialism

Allende wanted to set Chile on a course of peaceful but extreme changes, a program that he called the Chilean Road to Socialism. Soon after taking office, he called for a completely socialist economy—in other words, he wanted to do away with all private ownership of land and industry—and he established full diplomatic relations with Communist and Socialist countries such as Cuba and the People's Republic of China. He also wanted to give unused land to peasants and to do away with social classes by distributing wealth evenly.

From the beginning of his presidency, Allende had trouble achieving these goals. He was supported by a coalition, or group of six different parties that had pooled their votes to get him elected; the members of the coalition, however, often disagreed on just how far down the road to socialism they wanted to travel. Allende spent government money to increase the number of jobs and raise wages, but when wages rose, prices rose also for two reasons: first, because people had more money to spend on a limited number of products, and second, because higher wages increased the cost of producing goods. Prices skyrocketed; between 1971 and 1973, the rate of inflation increased from 22 percent to 508 percent—which meant that each peso lost its buying power about 25 times faster in 1973 than it had in 1971.

More members of Allende's coalition were elected to Congress in 1971 and 1972, but by 1973, Allende was losing the support of the PDC, the Roman Catholic church, and the middle class. In addition, Allende's government was undermined to some degree by a right-wing plan to sabotage the national economy by manipulating workers to call strikes or slowdowns in agricultural and industrial production. Copper workers, professional workers, and truck owners went on strike, not suspecting that some of the strikes had been set up by opponents of Allende in order to discredit him.

One week before Allende was overthrown in a coup, throngs of middle-class women joined farm laborers, truck drivers, copper miners, and others protesting the dizzying rate of inflation under Allende's coalition government.

U.S. Interference

In addition to this internal resistance, Allende encountered opposition from the U.S. government. The United States opposed Allende both because of his Marxism and because he planned to nationalize, or seize ownership of, American-owned copper mines in Chile without paying the American companies anything. U.S. interference in Chilean politics is known to have taken place in the 1960s, when the U.S. Central Intelligence Agency (CIA) contributed at least $3 million to Frei's campaign to ensure that he would beat Allende. In 1970, the United States again tried to prevent Allende from winning. Once he was elected, however, U.S. opposition continued.

The United States was the leader of a group of nations and international financial organizations that refused to make loans to Chile or to invest in the country. Furthermore, U.S. congressional hearings have shown that the United States secretly encouraged some of the anti-Allende strikes and marches in Chile and also supported certain anti-Allende organizations, including extreme right-wing groups such as Fatherland and Liberty, which called for strong military control of the government. The CIA may have given as much as $8 million in aid to anti-Allende groups. The CIA had help from the International Telephone and Telegraph Corporation (ITT), which had a large investment in Chile's telephone company. Because ITT feared that the telephone company would be nationalized the way the mines had been, the American company gave another $1 million to the anti-Allende organizations. These organizations, in turn, urged the armed forces to take power from Allende, who had lost all control of the military.

Pinochet Comes to Power

On September 11, 1973, the military seized control in a coup. Major General Augusto Pinochet Ugarte, whom Allende had recently appointed to head the army, joined leaders of the other branches of the armed forces in demanding that the president resign. On the morning of the coup, a Chilean air force general offered Allende a plane that would take him out of Chile and into exile. Allende replied, "The president of Chile does not flee in a plane." In a radio speech he said, "I am ready to resist by any means, even at the cost of my life, so that this may serve as a lesson in the ignominious history of those who use force, not reason." *Ignominious* means "disgraceful," and Allende was referring to Chile's national motto, By Reason or by Force.

Although Allende survived the explosion of 18 air force rockets that severely damaged the presidential palace, he died when troops later stormed La Moneda. The new government insisted that Allende committed suicide but refused to release photographs of the scene of his death, and some people believe that Allende was actually executed by the military. The truth may never be known.

Just hours after the storming of La Moneda, a four-member ruling junta, consisting of the chiefs of the armed services and the *carabineros* (national police) and led by Pinochet, had taken control of the government. The junta ordered the nation's legislators to disband, dissolving Congress for the first time in the 150-year history of independent Chile. It then issued a "decree-law" naming itself the sole government.

One week after the coup, mourners march past iron crosses that mark the graves of Allende supporters and other victims of the 1973 violence.

The new government outlawed the activities and publications of all political parties; it outlawed the very existence of the Socialist and Communist parties. The junta also suspended civil liberties, censored the press, and brutally repressed all politicians who had had anything to do with Allende, as well as labor leaders, university professors, and anyone suspected of being a Marxist. In what it called a "holy war" against Marxism, the military junta arrested as many as 90,000 people, or 1 in every 125 Chilean adults. At least 2,500 people died in, or soon after, the coup; the death total is probably closer to 10,000, although some anti-Pinochet groups claim that it could be as high as 80,000. Thousands more were tortured, threatened, or imprisoned without trial. The mutilated victims were sometimes dumped in rivers or left on street corners as a warning to others. Some Chileans disappeared entirely, their bodies buried in secret graves or dropped into the ocean.

The case of Lucho Alvarado, former director of a public agency that provided housing for the poor, was typical. Three weeks after the coup, the carabineros arrested him and took him to the National Stadium, where thousands of others were also being held. Like most of the prisoners, Alvarado was tortured for days. He was then shipped to a concentration camp in the northern desert and held there for nine months.

In a statement soon after the coup, Pinochet recalled that "Chile was one of the first countries in the world to abolish slavery." Now, he said, "our country has broken the chains of totalitarian Marxism, the great Twentieth Century Slavery. . . . We are thus once again pioneers in Humanity's fight for liberation."

In the aftermath of the 1973 coup, suspected leftists herded into the National Stadium watch their carabinero *guards instead of a soccer game. Many of the prisoners were tortured for days and then sent to distant detention camps.*

Government and Society

The military government that came to power in the coup of 1973 continued to rule Chile through the 1980s. The initial four-man junta gave way to the personal dictatorship of Pinochet, who took the title commander in chief of the army and president of the republic.

During the coup, the junta declared Chile to be in a state of siege; this state lasted until 1978, when it was replaced by the slightly less serious state of emergency. Both states, however, allowed the military to suspend the constitution in favor of martial law, which gives the military sole power to interpret and enforce the laws. Although some parts of the constitutional government, such as the courts, remained in operation, the junta crippled them by removing officials who did not agree with the junta's policies. The Office of the Comptroller General, a powerful, independent agency that had been created to oversee the government budget and rule on the constitutionality of laws, was weakened when it lost its power to help Congress impeach cabinet members—that is, to try them for crimes committed while in office.

Under the junta, military officers took over all key responsibilities. Although the 1925 constitution was not scrapped at once, the junta declared that its own decree-laws would take the place of constitutional law.

In keeping with their right-wing belief that government should have a limited role in society and the economy, Chile's new rulers cut the size and scope of the government. Government spending on public programs fell almost 18 percent between 1974 and 1979. One-fifth of all government-sponsored jobs were eliminated, and 100,000 jobs, mostly in state-operated corporations, disappeared by 1980. CORFO, the industrial development corporation, which had taken control of many nationalized industries during Allende's presidency, was reduced from 6,000 to 800 employees by 1977, and most of the 500 companies it controlled were returned to private owners.

Assassinations, executions, disappearances, exile, and torture remained common in Chile from 1973 through 1978. After 1978, the Pinochet government began to hide these activities more carefully. Government spokespeople claimed that victims died during riots or illegal confrontations with the police. But the Chilean Human Rights Commission reported that from 1981 to 1985 alone there were 306 political killings, 1,119 reports of torture, and 3,547 reports of cruel and inhuman treatment.

A new constitution written by the Pinochet government was approved in a 1980 plebiscite; this plebiscite, however, appears to have been fraudulent. No lists of registered voters were used to prevent government supporters from voting more than once, blank ballots were counted as votes in favor of the constitution, and Pinochet officials were responsible for all vote counting.

Fraudulent or not, the 1980 constitution allowed Pinochet to remain president through 1997, but it also called for another plebiscite in 1988. It was possible that Pinochet could be voted out of office in this plebiscite, although he would be the only candidate. A

Eight suspected Communists accused of plotting to assassinate Pinochet await trial. The secret police used black hoods to keep prisoners from knowing where they were being held.

new National Congress, with some members elected by the people and some appointed by Pinochet, would resume legislative functions in 1990, and a free presidential election would be held in 1997. The constitution also legalized censorship of the press, limits on free assembly, imprisonment of political prisoners without charges or trials, exile of the government's opponents, and the suspension of political parties and the disbanding of Congress.

The Chilean economy improved during the first several years of Pinochet's term, but this progress came to a sudden halt with a deep recession, or overall decline in spending and production, in 1982. By 1983, Chile owed more money to foreign banks, per person, than any country in the world. Since then, Chile's economy has failed to improve greatly, reports of torture and murder have continued, and the opposition to Pinochet has grown to include as many as 18 political parties, all of whom agree that democracy must be restored.

The first reported attempt on Pinochet's life occurred in 1986 when an automobile procession in which he was riding was attacked by a group equipped with automatic weapons and rocket launchers. Five bodyguards were killed and 11 others seriously wounded, but Pinochet received only a cut on his left hand. The furious president imposed a new state of siege during which four innocent people, including an anti-Pinochet journalist, were killed. In 1987, 12 people accused of being involved in the assassination plot were killed in neighborhood raids by Pinochet's police spies, the National Information Center (CNI).

Around this time, the U.S. government began objecting to the state of affairs in Chile. In July 1986, a Chilean-born American citizen was burned to death by soldiers during a protest in Santiago. This incident, together with the continuing state of siege and the 14-year accumulation of reports about violations of the civil rights of Chilean citizens, led U.S. president Ronald Reagan to call on other governments to support a UN resolution that condemned Chile's human rights record as one of the worst in the world.

On October 5, 1988, the plebiscite that had been promised in the 1980 constitution took place. Because the constitution had specified that no other candidate would be allowed to run in the plebiscite, Pinochet claimed that the choice was between him and chaos. But

By 1983, Chileans were once again looking at high prices for everyday goods. Many were also unemployed after the economy crumbled in 1981–82.

a well-organized group of opposition parties convinced voters that their coalition could provide a democratic alternative to Pinochet. The same opposition group ensured the fairness of the plebiscite with poll watchers and computerized vote-counting machines. Asked whether Pinochet should remain president through 1997, 55 percent of Chilean voters said no. Because of the no vote, Pinochet scheduled a presidential election for December 4, 1989, and promised to give up the presidency by March 1990, although he retained the ability to remain commander in chief of the army for some years to come.

Structure of the Government

Since taking the title of president in 1974, Pinochet has been able to make many decisions without consulting the other members of the junta. He has been assisted in his control of the government by a number of government ministries, or departments, each headed by a cabinet minister, and also by civilian and military advisers. He relies chiefly upon a presidential staff that coordinates the work of the ministries, a presidential advisory committee that writes all new laws, and a national security council that deals with military affairs. A powerless body called the Council of State was created in 1976 to give the impression that the people's interests are represented in this authoritarian government.

The only branch of the government that has prospered since the coup is the armed forces, which have expanded in both budget and staff. The total staff of the armed forces increased from 60,000 in 1973 to 97,000 in 1981. By the early 1980s, at least 21 percent of the government's annual budget went to the military. The armed forces consist of an army, a navy, and an air force. The president appoints the commanders of all three services and also may order their retirement.

In addition to the 3 armed forces, the paramilitary national police force, the carabineros, numbers about 27,000 men, all vol-

Women have had the right to vote since 1949 but must vote separately. Like other Chilean voters, they showed their power when they voted against Pinochet in the 1988 plebiscite.

unteers. They are trained in the use of tear gas, grenades, and water cannons. Another branch of the police is called the Investigative Police. It consists of 2,500 to 3,500 plainclothes policemen who cooperate with the carabineros and the armed forces. Like some of the carabineros, the Investigative Police have been accused of abusing police power. In 1980, several of them helped cause riots and other violent incidents that were designed to look like anti-Pinochet terrorism so that the government could justify its repression of its opponents.

Although the 1980 constitution guarantees citizens life, liberty, and the right to privacy, such rights are often violated in practice. Police may enter homes, seize property, and make arrests without charges or warrants if they claim to be combating crime (a phrase that is interpreted to mean many things) or during a state of national emergency (which occurs quite often).

Chile's chief espionage and information-gathering agency is the secret police organization called the National Information Center (CNI). It was founded by the junta under the name National Intelligence Directorate (DINA), but DINA became so notorious for torture and brutality that Pinochet fired its director, abolished the organization, and established it again under the new name. DINA and CNI have been accused of murder, arresting people without cause, torture and other forms of cruel and degrading treatment in prison, secret executions, and the provocation of shootouts with leftists in order to execute them. The secret police became internationally notorious in 1976 when they were accused of assassinating Orlando Letelier in Washington, D.C., by means of a bomb planted in his car. Letelier was a former Chilean ambassador and supporter of Allende. Chile has refused to extradite three of its government officials—that is, to send them to Washington to stand trial for the Letelier killing. The secret police have also been blamed for the death of Carlos Prats, Allende's army chief of staff, and for a near-fatal attack on Bernardo Leighton, leader of the Christian Democratic party.

After taking power, the junta promised to respect the authority of Chile's judicial system. The courts have continued to function, but all judges are appointed by Pinochet, and their positions and promotion depend on their political loyalties. Under Chilean law, defendants are tried not by juries but by the judges alone. Judges rely heavily upon police reports of the crime; if these reports are false, the accused person has little chance of a fair trial. District courts hear all minor criminal cases. More serious cases are heard in 11 courts of appeal. The 13-member Supreme Court, appointed by the president, is the final court of appeal. The Supreme Court also has some power to rule on whether laws are constitutional, but this power was greatly reduced by the 1980 constitution.

Perhaps the strongest blow against the judicial system came when it was stripped of authority over political cases. From 1973 to 1980, the cases of people who were charged by the government with committing political crimes were handled by military courts or by courts specially appointed by the government. Many political cases are still handled in this manner.

For the administration of regional and local government, each of Chile's 13 regions is headed by an *intendente*, or "manager." The regions are subdivided into a total of 42 provinces, each headed by a governor. The president appoints all the intendentes and governors from the ranks of military officers. The provinces are in turn subdivided into *comunas*, or "municipalities," each of which is headed by a subdelegate who is appointed by the provincial governor. City government is handled by councils of *regidores*, or "aldermen," who are elected by the citizens. The mayors of cities with more than 100,000 people, however, are appointed by the president.

Education

Chile has long been proud of its educational system, which was organized during the mid-19th century and was influenced chiefly by French teaching methods. Throughout the country's history, Chilean leaders have recognized the importance of education and have encouraged developments in the science of teaching. Even today, after upheavals in the organization and structure of the educational system, the government claims that Chile has an extraordinarily high literacy rate—96 percent of all Chileans over the age of 10 can read and write.

After 1973, the Pinochet government stated that the goal of education was to create "good workers, good citizens, and good patriots." Civilian authorities in all levels of the school system were replaced by military ones. The minister of education, supported by

Protesters jammed the Supreme Court building in 1983 to demand the release of a leader of the Christian Democratic party who opposed Pinochet.

the commander of the military institutes, removed from the schools books that discussed class divisions in society and recommended books that discussed Chilean history in an approving, noncontroversial manner. Pinochet and the junta made it clear that Chilean education should encourage Christian beliefs, patriotism, and respect for the family and should discourage all forms of Marxism and Communism.

Chile has four educational levels: preprimary, primary, secondary, and university. Preprimary education includes infant, toddler, and kindergarten programs. All children between 6 and 14 years old are required by law to attend the 8-year primary program, and this level has the largest number of students. Students who choose to do so may go on to the secondary level, which is a four-year program in either the sciences and humanities or technical and professional training.

Before 1973, Chile's universities were famous throughout Latin America. The University of Chile and the University of Santiago are located in Santiago and have branches in many cities around the country. There are several Catholic universities as well. Since the Pinochet coup, the universities have been transformed along with the rest of Chilean society. The persecution of Marxists and other leftists resulted in the firing of 30 percent of all professors and the expulsion of 10 to 15 percent of all students. Government funding has been cut, military officers have replaced academic administrators, and the government has abolished whole departments of social science, philosophy, political science, and education.

Two decree-laws handed down in January 1981 had important effects on the university system. One required for the first time that tuition be paid at public universities, so that low-income students could attend only if they obtained a government loan. The other decree-law reduced the variety of academic degrees that could be offered by universities, so that degrees in the arts, journalism, so-

Cuts in government spending for health and child care have hit the children in Santiago's shantytowns especially hard.

ciology, and philosophy are now given by institutes that do not have the status of universities.

Health Care

Government involvement in health care began with laws to regulate working conditions in the 1920s. In 1952, the National Health Service (SNS) was formed to control various government programs related to health. Its purpose was to provide health care to working-class and poor people. The SNS succeeded in improving public health in Chile, as measured by life expectancy and infant mortality. Life expectancy indicates how many years the average person will live; this figure has increased since the 1950s to 67.1 years. The infant mortality rate indicates how many of every 1,000 babies born will die in infancy. That figure was 147 in 1948; today it is 22. Overall improvements do not always tell the whole story, however. Infant mortality in some rural regions and in poor neighborhoods of Santiago and other cities has remained higher than in middle-class or wealthy areas.

Since 1973, the government has generally cut spending on health care. Before the coup, SNS provided free care to about two-thirds of all Chileans. After 1980, those served by SNS were offered private care, for which the government would pay a part of the cost. Because this system encourages all but the very poor to choose private care, the SNS system that remained to serve those poor was neglected and allowed to deteriorate.

In recent years, about 15 percent of Chile's physicians have left the country for jobs elsewhere. This fact, added to the breakdown of SNS services, has created shortages of doctors and medicine in public clinics. Patients often must face long delays for appointments and operations. Chile presently has 1 doctor for every 1,043 people and a total of 33,000 hospital beds for a population of more than 12 million. Charitable and religious organizations have tried to meet people's needs by opening clinics, but these are generally over-crowded.

Between the mid-1960s and 1979, both Allende and Pinochet supported population control, and the SNS operated one of the most effective birth-control programs in Latin America. Since then, however, the declining birthrate has alarmed government leaders, who now favor population growth. New laws make it difficult to obtain birth-control materials, and abortion is illegal.

Pinochet and the SNS claim to have achieved great success in eliminating malnutrition in Chile. Independent researchers at the University of Chile claim, however, that the government has under-estimated the rate of malnutrition by 50 to 65 percent. Widespread protein shortages, in particular, are believed to have caused an un-usually high rate of mental retardation.

Only 250,000 pure-blooded Araucanians remain in Chile, but 80 percent of all Chileans can claim some Indian ancestors.

People and Culture

Most Chileans today are descended from the Spanish colonists and Indians who intermixed during the colonial era. The Indians were the Araucanians; the Spanish came chiefly from Spain's Andalusia, Estremadura, Castile, and León provinces. Basques—people from the western Pyrenees Mountains on the border between Spain and France—followed the first wave of settlement; many of the Basques became merchants or bought up the lands that the Jesuits had owned before they were driven from the country in 1767. The 80 percent of all Chileans who are descended from both Spanish/Basque and Indian ancestors are called *mestizos*.

The mestizos had begun to play an important part in Chilean society by the end of the 17th century. They were heirs of the original *encomenderos* (landholders), artisans, and overseers of ranches. Today they share a strong sense of cultural unity. Almost all speak Spanish, Chile's official language, and are members of the Roman Catholic church. In some Latin American countries a small, privileged mestizo class dominates a large Indian population, but the numerous mestizos are the base of Chilean society. They are dominated by a much smaller class whose members are primarily of European descent; this European class controls most business and government. The Europeans are mostly of Spanish descent, but some are French, Italian, German, English, or Yugoslavian.

Immigrants and Indians

Although fewer people from around the world have emigrated to Chile than to some other countries in South America, Chile has experienced several distinct waves of immigrants after the initial Spanish/Basque conquest and settlement.

English, Irish, and Scottish miners and merchants arrived throughout the 18th and 19th centuries. Like the Basques, most of them quickly became part of the Chilean elite class; many of them married into Spanish families.

From 1800 to about 1850, a large number of Germans settled in the south, especially around Puerto Montt. Many people in that region speak German today, and German names and customs have been preserved.

Around 1900, a number of people from Spain, Italy, Switzerland, Yugoslavia, Jordan, Syria, and Lebanon came to Chile to trade, to establish small businesses, or to seek their fortunes in the rumored goldfields of Tierra del Fuego (which proved to contain no gold). Many of the disappointed gold seekers entered the ranching and fishing industries; most moved to other parts of the country, but a few thousand of their descendants still live in Porvenir, the only large town in the bleak, windswept Chilean portion of Tierra del Fuego.

The most recent wave of immigration into Chile came in the years just before and after Allende's election in 1970. About 10,000 political refugees from Brazil, Argentina, and Bolivia fled to Chile to escape persecution by their own governments. After Pinochet came to power in 1973, most of these immigrants were expelled from Chile.

The smallest ethnic group in Chile today is the Indian population. About 250,000 pure-blooded Araucanians remain; nearly all are Mapuche. They speak their own language, which is understood by few non-Indian Chileans. They also share the belief that the Mapuche—which means "people of the land"—are the rightful owners of most of Chile and that the rest of the Chileans have stolen their land. The government of Chile succeeded in winning the area south of the Bío-Bío River from the Mapuche in the late 19th century, after the War of the Pacific. It then forced the Indians to move onto reservations. By 1929, Chilean landowners had acquired about 22.2 million of the 24.7 million acres that had been owned by the Mapuche (9 million of 10 million hectares). In recent years, the Pinochet government has given some Mapuche legal ownership of the meager parcels of reservation land on which they live, but poverty has forced many of these Indians to sell their newly acquired property to nearby landowners.

Chilean Social Classes

At the top of Chilean society is a small, powerful elite class that consists mostly of descendants of European immigrants. Members of this class often own large investments in the giant diversified corporations that control much of Chile's financial and economic activity. These investments have given the elite class an unusual ability to prosper, even after many of the largest estates were broken up by Allende's land-reform laws. When the military junta began

This 1890 photograph shows Mapuche living much as they had for centuries. Only after Chile had won the War of the Pacific in 1883 did it achieve complete dominance over the Mapuche in the south.

selling the companies that had been nationalized by Allende back to private owners, members of this class had cash available to buy them.

Immigrant families in Chile typically improved their social status over the generations. An immigrant would try to marry into a Chilean family of good status, to accumulate some money, and then to buy land. Members of the next generation would add agricultural, mining, and merchant businesses to the family wealth and would often marry into the wealthiest families of the true elite. Third-generation immigrants then reinforced their elite status through marriage; many of them held public office.

Below the elite on the social ladder is Chile's middle class, which contains both European and mestizo individuals. Only during the 20th century has this group emerged as prosperous and important. It includes many small landowners and small business owners, construction supervisors, government employees, technicians, and industrial managers. By 1970, the middle class accounted for more than one-third of the working population.

Among middle-class people, those with a shared ethnic background or those who work in the same profession frequently organize into clubs or professional societies called *gremios*. In general, these gremios opposed Allende and supported the military junta. Since the late 1970s, however, the middle class has suffered from Chile's economic recessions and stagnation. People have lost their jobs or their businesses, had their wages held down, or been denied insurance and other benefits from the government. The results of the 1988 plebiscite show that the large middle class is no longer happy with Pinochet's management of the country.

Chile's lower class is mostly mestizo. It includes factory workers, farm laborers on big estates, skilled workers in unions, peasants who work on their own small farms, copper and coal miners, and crafts workers. The poor and unemployed are usually included in this social class.

Pope John Paul II visited Chile for four days in 1987. At the National Sanctuary of Maipu he crowned a statue known as the Virgin del Carmen. Like most nations originally settled by the Spanish, Chile has a predominantly Roman Catholic population.

About 83 percent of Chile's population live in cities or towns; 17 percent live in the countryside, mostly on farms. Chile has a population density of 43 people per square mile (17 per square kilometer); this is low compared to the population densities of many nations, but some parts of Chile, such as the capital city, have very high densities. The central valley is the most populated part of the country; the north, the south, the Andes Mountains, and the coastal cordillera are the least populated.

Religion

In terms of religious affiliation, 82 percent of Chileans identify themselves as Roman Catholic. Chile also has a higher share of Protestants than any other predominantly Roman Catholic country in Latin America. Some are Anglicans and Lutherans, the descendants of British and German immigrants who came to Chile in the 19th century. Most Protestants, however, especially those in the working class, belong to fundamentalist churches (sects that emphasize the personal relationship between God and humanity).

The Roman Catholic majority displays a fervent commitment to Catholic values, even though most people do not attend formal religious services. Practices of worship also vary by class and geographic region. People in Santiago are more likely to attend Mass than those in outlying areas, and Catholics in the upper class are much more likely to attend Mass than those in the working class.

The position and influence of the Catholic church in Chile has changed over time. During the 19th century priests often used their position to reinforce the existing economic and political order. In some of their sermons, for example, they told farm laborers that obedience, submission to authority, and tradition were the virtues that should guide workers' lives.

The Catholic church in Chile changed its attitude on social issues beginning in the 1930s, when, inspired by papal encyclicals (documents issued by the pope), church officials began to emphasize social reform as a Christian duty. During the 1950s and 1960s, Jesuit priest Alberto Hurtado helped educate rising politicians about social issues, and conservative Catholics were surprised to find that Catholic bishops did not oppose the birth-control policies implemented in the 1960s. However, the increasing activity of the church on behalf of the working class and the poor caused it to lose influence with members of the upper class.

Since the 1973 coup, the church has played an important role in alerting people to the firings, arrests, and disappearances that have marked military rule. At the same time, it has tried to com-

When Pablo Neruda won the Nobel Prize for literature in 1971, he was serving as Allende's ambassador to France.

pensate for government cuts in social spending. The church has opened health clinics, provided a hot-lunch program for about 30,000 Santiago children, helped small farmers form cooperative organizations, and provided financial aid to the press and to organizations that are researching the various effects of military rule.

The Arts and Cultural Life

In contrast to the complex ruins left by the Incas and Aztecs of Peru and Mexico, the Chilean Indians left little behind other than crude tools and simple burial sites. The Mapuche, their descendants, continue to practice some folk-art traditions such as ceramics, weaving, and making handicrafts from horsehair. However, most of Chile's arts and literature are in the European tradition, despite the large numbers of mestizo Chileans who share the Indian heritage. Chile's culture and art are basically derived from Hispanic sources.

Chile has been home to many fine writers but is perhaps most proud of its poets. *La Araucana*, the epic poem written at the end of the 16th century by Alonso de Ercilla y Zúñiga (1534–94), describes the bravery of the Indians resisting Spanish conquistadores; some people consider it the greatest Latin American epic poem. In the 19th century several exiles from other South American nations found refuge in Chile and inspired Chilean writers. Rubén Darío, a Nicaraguan poet who is sometimes considered the father of modern Latin American literature, settled in Chile in 1886 and influenced numerous writers. The most famous native Chilean poets are Gabriela Mistral (1889–1957), who in 1945 became the first Latin American winner of the Nobel Prize for literature, and Pablo Neruda (1904–73), who won the Nobel Prize for literature in 1971. Neruda was not only a well-known poet but also a diplomat and national hero. He served as a senator and filled several consulships and ambassadorships; some leftists even suggested that he run instead of Allende as a presidential candidate in 1970.

Another world-renowned Chilean is the pianist Claudio Arrau, who is especially noted for his performances of works by Beethoven. But classical music is by no means the only sort heard in Chile. Many types of folk music accompany traditional dancing—both are essential ingredients of almost all celebrations, which are often related to Catholic feast days or harvest festivities. Traditional instruments vary by region and include the *guitarrón*, which has 25 strings and is shaped like a guitar but is much bigger. In the northern altiplanos the *queña*, a flute made of a single reed, and the *zampoña*, a pipe made of reeds of different lengths bound with bright wool, are popular. The Mapuche in the south play the *kultrum*, a type of drum, and the *trutruca*, a wind instrument made of a long piece of bamboo.

A few of these instruments, along with a violin, may accompany the guitar in the music for the *cueca*, Chile's national dance. Couples dance the cueca together, waving a handkerchief in elaborate patterns. The man may sometimes wear the traditional outfit of the huaso. Huasos were the cowboys of Chile—romantic figures who herded cattle on the northern altiplanos and in the central valley in the 1800s. Their costume consists of a broad-brimmed black hat, a short, elaborately embroidered cape, or poncho, a brightly colored waist sash, and tight, high-waisted trousers pulled over boots adorned with delicate, ornate silver spurs. Huasos are also responsible for another time-honored Chilean tradition—the rodeo, a contest in which huasos competed to show off their horsemanship.

Chilean cuisine varies from region to region. On the coast Chileans enjoy a wide range of fish and shellfish, including sea bass, eels, sole, abalone, clams, sea urchins, crabs, shrimp, mussels, and lobsters. Beef is a less important source of protein, and mutton, pork, and chicken are more popular. Delicious specialties include *empanadas*, triangular pastries filled with *pino*, a mixture of chopped meat, onions, eggs, and raisins; *pastel de choclo*, a dish consisting

The spirited cueca *is Chile's national dance. A cueca competition is held each June in Arica.*

of a layer of pino and a layer of cooked chicken covered with a sweet, herb-flavored corn soufflé; and *humitas,* mashed sweet corn kernels flavored with basil, wrapped in corn husks, and boiled.

Chile's geography provides many opportunities for sports and recreation. The resort of Viña del Mar on the coast caters to sun-bathers and water-sports enthusiasts, whereas the Andes in the north and the volcanoes of the south provide steep slopes for skiers. The national sport, however, is soccer. There are 36 professional teams and numerous amateur and semiprofessional players.

Cultural institutions in the capital city include the Museum of Fine Arts, with a permanent display of works by Chilean artists, the Municipal Theater, and the National Library, the largest in South America.

Chile is one of the world's leading producers of fish meal and fish oil, and many Chileans hope to expand the fishing industry. Considering the nation's 2,610 miles (4,200 kilometers) of coast, the potential for growth is great.

Economy, Transportation, and Communications

Chile has rich natural resources that it has exploited thoroughly in spite of the country's rough terrain. From independence until the War of the Pacific (1879–83), Chile relied on agricultural exports from the central valley and on mining products from Norte Chico. After the war, when Chile obtained profitable nitrate fields from Peru and Bolivia, the economy relied almost totally on nitrate exports until World War I, when an artificial substitute for nitrate was developed and the price for natural nitrate collapsed.

After the nitrate boom ended, mining companies began to emphasize copper. Chile holds about 20 percent of the world's copper reserves, mostly in the Norte Grande and Norte Chico and along the Andes from Concepción through the central part of the country. Iron and molybdenum (a metal produced during copper refining, of which Chile is the world's largest supplier) are its next most common metals. High-quality iron deposits in Norte Chico and along the coast have proved to be important exports. Other deposits found in Chile include gold, silver, manganese, lead, zinc, mercury, apatite (used in making phosphate fertilizers), limestone, marble, and gypsum.

The country's other significant natural resource is its vast forests, which cover 21 percent of the country. South of the Bío-Bío River, the rainy climate favors the growth of natural forests, which are sources of hardwoods and building lumber. Soft lumber for use in making paper also is taken from rapid-growth or cultivated forests in this region and from forests in central Chile.

Among energy sources, Chile has coal, petroleum, and natural gas deposits as well as tremendous potential for generating power in hydroelectric plants. The National Electric Company (Empresa Nacional de Electricidad) has set up hydroelectric plants in the Andes and the coastal mountain range at a number of locations. Soft coal exists in underwater deposits in the Arauco Gulf, south of Concepción. Some oil and gas is extracted on Tierra del Fuego and along the north shore of the Strait of Magellan, but this meets only one-fourth of the nation's annual oil requirements.

The Chilean economy today depends primarily on exports of minerals, especially copper, which the late president Salvador Allende called "the wage of Chile." Some light industrial products are manufactured within Chile, but the basic fact about Chile's economy—that its health hinges on uninterrupted production of raw materials and stable world prices for those materials—has not changed greatly in a century of economic development.

Chile's chief exports remain copper ores and refined and unrefined copper, which account for about 40 percent of the country's export earnings. Its remaining exports include other metals, fruits and vegetables, fish meal, paper and paper products, and chemical and petroleum products. Principal importers of Chilean products include West Germany, the United States, Japan, and Brazil.

Manufactured goods, primarily machinery and automobiles and other forms of transport equipment, are Chile's chief import. In addition, Chile imports fuels and other energy sources, food and agricultural raw materials, certain chemical products, and many luxury items and consumer goods. The United States supplies about one-quarter of Chile's import needs, followed by Japan, Brazil, and West Germany.

Although mining is Chile's primary economic activity, the country also manufactures many important products that are consumed at home. Among these are cement, cellulose, and sugar, as well as such miscellaneous items as newsprint, detergent, margarine, beverages, and tires. Services such as banking, teaching, and insurance employ 35 percent of Chile's work force. Manufacturing and construction employ another 19 percent; the combined trade, hotel, and restaurant industries also employ 19 percent of workers. Eighteen percent have jobs in agriculture, forestry, or fishing. Nine percent work in other fields.

Mining is the mainstay of the Chilean economy. The copper industry was developed by large North American investments during the first few decades of the 20th century. Until the 1960s, two U.S. companies owned the mines that produced 90 percent of Chile's copper. In 1971, the Allende government nationalized many foreign

Workers prepare a blast furnace for firing in order to extract metal from ore. Many of the mineral ores Chile exports, however, are refined in other countries.

copper operations, and today mines run by the National Copper Corporation (CODELCO-Chile) produce the bulk of Chile's copper output. Copper ore is mined along with other materials through strip-mining (such as at the vast open-pit copper mine of Chuquicamata, first excavated by the Incas) or through tunneling. The ore is then converted to copper by electrolysis or "blistering" (fire refining). The final product is sent to northern ports such as Antofagasta, Barquito, and San Antonio to be shipped overseas.

Though the government has retained control over mineral operations in copper, coal, nitrates, and iron ore, the National Planning Office (ODE-PLAN) has encouraged private investors, both foreign and Chilean, to invest in the expansion of natural resource development in petroleum and natural gas. The office emphasizes natural-resource development by foreign as well as Chilean investors. New laws in 1977 and 1981 were designed to attract foreign investment in Chile's mining industry by lowering taxes on such investments and guaranteeing that foreign investors' rights would be protected.

Chilean agriculture employs 18 percent of the labor force but accounts for only 10 percent of the country's total domestic production. Because agriculture is not a highly developed part of the economy, Chile must import large amounts of food commodities. Its major products are sugar beets, wheat, grapes, potatoes, corn, apples, oats, and tomatoes. Nearly three-quarters of all grapes imported into the United States come from Chile. Meadows and pastures account for 16 percent of the land in Chile; cultivation accounts for 7 percent. Vineyards in the Mediterranean region of the country produce a variety of good wines. Livestock raising is the principal economic activity in many rural areas. Cattle are raised in the north and center and sheep in the south of the country. The dairy industry is growing, and recently new technologies have increased the production of beef, poultry, pork, and mutton.

Chile's substantial exports of grapes to the United States were cut back severely when terrorists poisoned a few grapes in a shipment in early 1989. Consumers' fears proved groundless, however, when no more problems were reported.

What industry there is in Chile is concentrated around the principal urban centers. Chile's light industrial products are primarily textiles, food products, and clothing. Plants in other parts of the country process sugar beets, produce cellulose and paper from lumber, and manufacture cement. The fish-meal industry produces fish meal (used as fertilizer and as food for livestock) and fish oil for export. A few plants in the north assemble electronic and other types of equipment, as well as automobiles. The large industrial complex at San Vicente in Concepción has grown tremendously since the Huachipato steelworks opened in 1950. Chile's second petroleum refinery and first petrochemical complex, built in 1970, are also located in San Vicente.

Changes in the Economy

The military claimed that it seized power in Chile in 1973 in part to restore prosperity. Since then, the economy has had its ups and downs, but in 1987, after more than 13 years of military rule, the total value of goods and services produced per person each year (per capita gross national product, or GNP) was no higher than it was in 1973. Income per person had fallen by 20 percent; purchasing, by 8 percent. Manufacturing had grown at a rate of only 1.1 percent per year, compared with the 4.1 percent yearly rate during the 8 years before the coup.

Pinochet's economic advisers believed they could best revive the economy by reducing the role of the government. The junta sold many of the businesses Allende had nationalized back to private owners—mainly to already wealthy Chileans and multinational corporations such as ITT—and reduced the high taxes on imported goods, many of which competed with goods produced by Chile's own industries. As a result of this competition, many small and middle-sized Chilean businesses failed. Unemployment in the middle and lower classes grew, and the growing population of jobless citizens was unable to buy many consumer goods, to save money, or to

Chilean industries include the processing and canning of shellfish. During the deep recession of 1981–82, such industries suffered and some went bankrupt, putting thousands of workers, including many women, out of work.

invest. New businesses had difficulty getting started, established industries struggled to remain successful, and the economy became stagnant.

The poor have been left out of the economic gains that have occurred since 1973. Income per person in Chile today is about U.S. $1,465 annually, but this does not take into account the flow of income from the very poor to the very rich, in a sort of reversal of the Robin Hood story. Whereas the richest 20 percent of Chileans have seen their incomes rise by almost one-third since 1970, the poorest 40 percent make about half what they did at that time. Minimum wages set by law were cut in half and continue to decline, and social spending has been cut by 20 percent since 1970, so that fewer and smaller government programs must help larger numbers of people.

The 1982 recession cost many lower-class and working-class laborers their jobs. Eleven percent of the work force is unemployed, but an additional 11 percent is underemployed—for example, former construction workers and factory supervisors are reduced to selling chocolate bars and coat hangers on downtown streets. Between 4 and 5 percent of workers, though employed, are in make-work jobs (jobs created by the government to employ people) in which they earn between U.S. $25 and U.S. $50 per month, about a third of what the average Chilean earns. Unemployment in some Santiago neighborhoods ranges from 40 percent to 60 percent, and 10,000 people rely on soup kitchens. More than a quarter of Chileans live in extreme poverty.

The Chilean economy recovered somewhat in the late 1980s. Foreign debt equaled 116 percent of the GNP in 1986; it was down to 83 percent in 1989. As Chile enters the 1990s, its economy may recover completely, continue to struggle, or falter again. Much depends on politics, because whatever faction or party gains political control in the 1989 election will control economic policy as well.

Transportation

Chile's geography limits communications and the flow of traffic throughout the country. The central valley is a natural path for both roads and railways, but it covers only a portion of the country. In the north, between Arica and Santiago, people use the Coastal Pan-American Highway more than the railroad, which is used primarily for carrying ores. South of Puerto Montt, where Chile's chain of islands begins, roads and railroads disappear, and travel is possible only by air or sea.

The Pan-American Highway is the country's main highway. It connects Arica with Chiloé Island, covering a distance of 2,100 miles (3,381 kilometers). Other major roads run between Santiago and the ports of San Antonio and Valparaíso. Construction of the Lo Prado Tunnel through the coastal cordillera has considerably shortened the route to Valparaíso. The most important international road in Chile connects Santiago with Mendoza, Argentina. Others connect Iquique with Oruro, Bolivia; Antofagasta with Salta, Argentina; La Serena with San Juan, Argentina; and Osorno in the Lake District with the ski resort town of San Carlos de Bariloche, Argentina.

In 1977, workers widened an important tunnel through the Andes that links the border towns of Caracoles, Chile, and Las Cuevas, Argentina. The pass, located about 52 miles northeast of Santiago, allows both railroad and highway traffic.

Santiago is well served by urban transportation, including public buses, subways, and private vehicles.

Chile has one of the better rail systems in South America. Run by the State Railway Company, its tracks cover about 4,000 miles (6,400 kilometers). It is really two systems, both electrified: a northern network running between La Calera and Iquique and a southern network between La Calera and Puerto Montt. Its most-traveled sections connect Santiago with Valparaíso and with Puerto Montt. The most important international rail line runs between Los Andes, Chile, and Mendoza, Argentina.

The sea is one road that runs along the entire country. In colonial days, all travel was by sea. Today, coastal shipping, formerly neglected, is growing in importance. The development of the Chilean national merchant marine and the modernization of the country's seaports have helped this trend. Government authorities, with the aid of private companies, supervise all sea transportation. Chile's busiest port of entry is Valparaíso. The country also has principal export centers at Huasco, Guayacán, and San Vicente, which are particularly involved with the shipping of minerals mined in Chile's northern region.

The Chilean National Airline (LAN-Chile) has almost total control of air transportation into and throughout the country. LAN-Chile connects Santiago with many South American capitals and many other countries.

Communications

Chile's great length and its mountain chains have made communications difficult for much of the country's history. Now an extensive telegraph network connects nearly all the cities and towns, and telephone service has expanded greatly in the past few decades. There were only 370,000 telephones in operation in the country in 1971; in 1989, there were 844,730, or 6.7 telephones for every 100 Chileans. However, most of these phones are in and around the capital, Santiago.

Both radio and television stations broadcast in Chile, but radio reaches many more Chileans than television does. Although by 1979 Chile had 1.22 million television sets and 1.5 million radios, the television sets were clustered in urban areas where good reception was possible, whereas radios could be found throughout the country. Most Chileans are within broadcast range of at least one of the 262 radio stations in Chile. Although the number of stations has increased since the coup, the variety of programs has not increased. In 1975, the Pinochet government closed several stations owned by leftists and political parties that had supported Allende. Television news is under state control as well, for the single nationwide television network is completely owned by the state.

Chile has had a long tradition of a politically active and fairly free press, but after the 1973 coup most newspapers and periodicals that were critical of the government were shut down. Journalists suspected of being Communists or Marxists were often imprisoned. But in the 1980s, the press ventured a little more criticism of the government but still faced occasional retaliation.

In October 1987, journalists marched through the streets of Santiago, demanding an end to censorship. In English, their banner proclaims, "Without freedom of expression there is no democracy."

The most important and broadly circulated daily newspapers and weekly magazines are published in Santiago and Valparaíso. The Santiago daily paper *El Mercurio* was founded in 1827 and claims to be the oldest newspaper in the Spanish-speaking world. (Its 1981 circulation was 325,000.) Other papers owned by the *El Mercurio* chain include two papers called *El Mercurio* published in Valparaíso (1981 circulation 100,000) and Antofagasta and two Santiago papers called *La Segunda* (1981 circulation 75,000) and *Las Últimas Noticias* (1981 circulation 85,000). The most popular paper in Santiago in 1981 was *La Tercera de la Hora*, with a circulation of 340,000. Widely read weekly magazines that publish national and international news include *Ercilla* and *¿Qué Pasa?*

Two leading opponents of Pinochet, Ricardo Lagos (left) and Patricio Aylwin, celebrate the results of the October 5, 1988, plebiscite. In the elections scheduled for 1989 and 1990, such leaders must present believable, attractive programs for government and assurances of political stability in order to gain power.

Chile's Future

Chile's history has been a history lived on the frontier. Founded by adventurers who despoiled the countryside and violently subjugated the native Mapuche, Chile was for years an intellectual and economic backwater, an outpost of the Spanish empire that was called a "cursed land without gold." Conquerors did not find gold and riches as they had in Mexico and Peru. They found a fiercely determined people with nothing to defend but their land, which they did with bravery and cunning for some 350 years. Surrounded by the natural barriers of the Atacama Desert to the north, the Pacific Ocean to the west, the Andes mountains to the east, and the warlike Mapuche to the south, the Spanish settlers were for many years confined to a tiny geographic area.

The history of Chile after its independence from Spain was shaped by the same realities. Unlike Argentina, a country to which European immigrants flocked during the 19th century, Chile attracted few immigrants. Those who did come were from upper-middle-class backgrounds and quickly became part of the ruling elite class. During the 19th century, Chile extended its borders through war with Peru and Bolivia, finally vanquished the Mapuche, and developed a system of government that, although easy for the ruling class to manipulate, at least guaranteed a measure of stability in a region known for its unruly politics.

But in the 20th century Chile found itself part of a modern world with modern achievements and problems. The country's artistic and cultural life was admired throughout Latin America and the world. Its educational and health-care systems worked well, and its pioneering social legislation was a model for other governments.

Against this background of apparent prosperity and good fortune, a growing number of workers were dissatisfied with their status. They clashed violently with an upper class that resented the economic progress being made by the lower classes. Political and economic chaos characterized the early 1970s, followed by the most repressive dictatorial regime in Chile's history as an independent nation. In a country with a tradition of respect for law and government and a high degree of tolerance for political debate and freedom of expression, social upheaval and violent military reprisal seemed out of place, but the all-encompassing nature of Pinochet's power has successfully transformed many of the institutions of Chilean society.

The presidential and congressional elections scheduled for 1989 and 1990 give Chile the opportunity to return to democratic government. Already the many Chilean parties that oppose Pinochet have begun to argue among themselves about who the presidential candidate should be. Although this is not unusual in Chile, some observers worry that the parties' tradition of squabbling may make it difficult for them to present an alternative to the turmoil of the last 15 years.

Chile's new president and Congress will have a large task ahead of them. The country's dependence on exporting natural resources has sometimes resulted in economic shocks when prices in the world markets for copper or nitrate changed dramatically. A new government will need to emphasize modernization of agriculture and industry. In addition, a new Chilean government must confront the problems of poverty and overcrowding in cities, particularly in Santiago, where the number of poor people living in *poblaciones* (shantytowns) is estimated at 1.5 million.

Chileans have always felt that they were unique among Latin Americans. Their saying *"No somos tropicales"* (roughly translated, "We're not like the rest of them") expresses the traditional attitude of Chileans toward the other Latin American nations. In many ways—geographically, ethnically, and politically—Chile *is* quite different from the rest of South America. Perhaps the future will restore to Chile the respect and admiration of its neighbors and the world.

Chileans weathered a number of political and economic storms in the 1960s, 1970s, and 1980s, but they face the future with a wealth of natural resources, optimism, and determination.

◄ G L O S S A R Y ►

Altiplanos Plateaus found in Norte Grande Region in Chile and to the northeast in Bolivia. High, wide, flat, and dry, they hold the majority of the mineral wealth that is the basis of Chile's economy.

Cabildos Town councils set up by Spanish colonial governors early in the conquest of South America.

Conquistadores Conquerors. Spanish soldiers and adventurers who undertook the first explorations of America and conquered Mexico and the Inca Empire in Peru as well as Chile.

Cordillera A system of mountain ranges. Chile has two such systems: the Cordillera Domeyko of the Andes Mountains on its eastern border and the coastal cordillera (Cordillera Patagónica), lower mountains that run down its western coast.

Coup A shortened form of the French phrase *coup d'état*, meaning a sudden seizure of political power.

Encomiendas Trusteeships granted by the early Spanish rulers of Chile to the military officers and other adventurers who accompanied them in the conquest.

Humboldt (Peru) Current A cold current of water flowing northeast from Antarctica along Chile's Pacific coast.

Inquilinos Laborers bound by debt to landowners in rural Chile.

Junta A ruling council or committee.

Llamas	Members of the camel family that are found in the Andean countries of South America (Bolivia, Chile, and Peru). Chile's dry northern plateaus are home to the llama (*Lama glama*), the alpaca (*Lama pacos*), and the vicuña (*Lama vicugna*).
Mapuche	The most numerous and well-known group of Indians in Chile, centered in present-day southern Chile at the time of the first Spanish explorations of the country. (Also called the Araucanians).
Mestizo	A person of mixed Indian and European descent and heritage.
Norte Chico	Little North. Chile's northernmost region until the War of the Pacific (1879–83), when Chile obtained the Atacama Desert from Peru and Bolivia.
Norte Grande	Great North. Representing about a third of Chile's area, but rather sparsely inhabited, this region contains the Atacama Desert, probably the world's driest.
Plebiscite	A vote in which an entire country or district votes on a proposal, especially having to do with a choice of political leadership.
Pudu	The world's smallest deer, generally rare, but found in a number of areas of Chile.
Reducciones	Community-owned parcels of land. The Jesuit order of the Catholic church organized Indians all over Spanish America into self-sufficient reducciones during the 1700s to prevent their enslavement.
Situado	A shortened form of *situado real* (royal subsidy). Money or provisions paid by the Spanish king through the viceroy of Peru to the Chilean government during the 17th century and the first half of the 18th century, for maintaining a government in Santiago and an army on the frontier to fight the Indians.

‹ I N D E X ›